PICTURE BOOK OF COUNTRY FARM LIFE

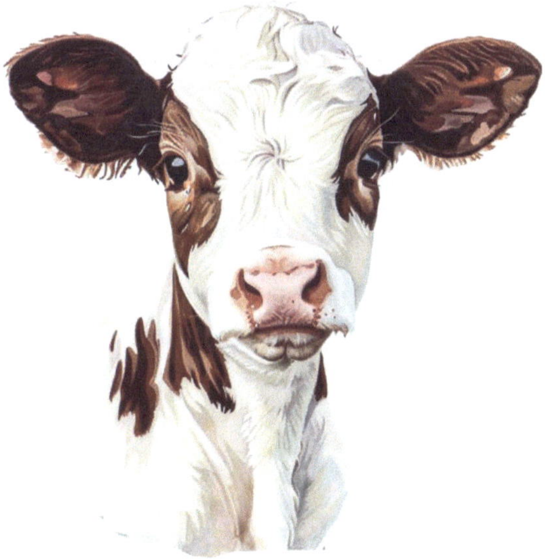

...By...

Ella Caldwell

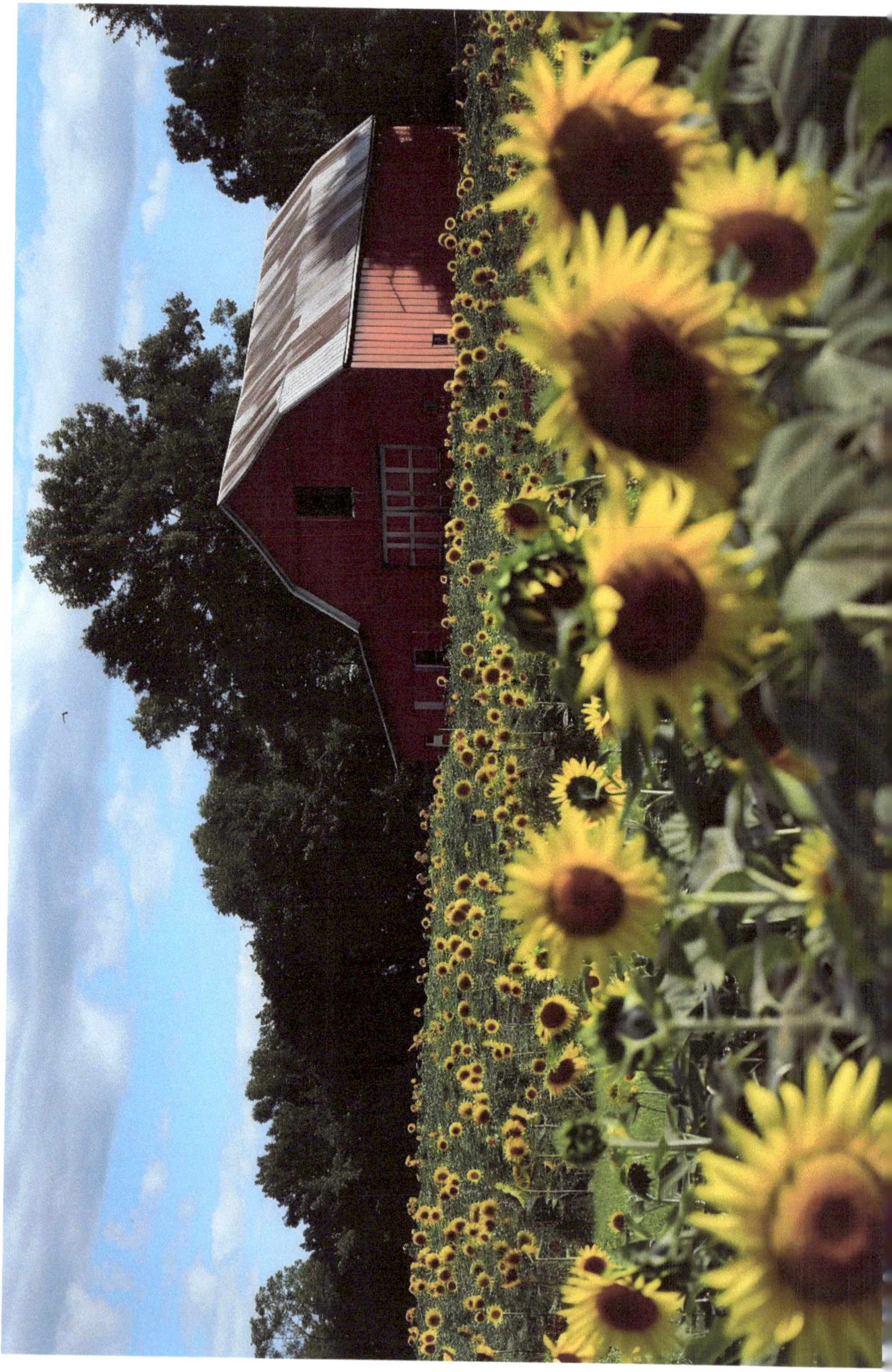

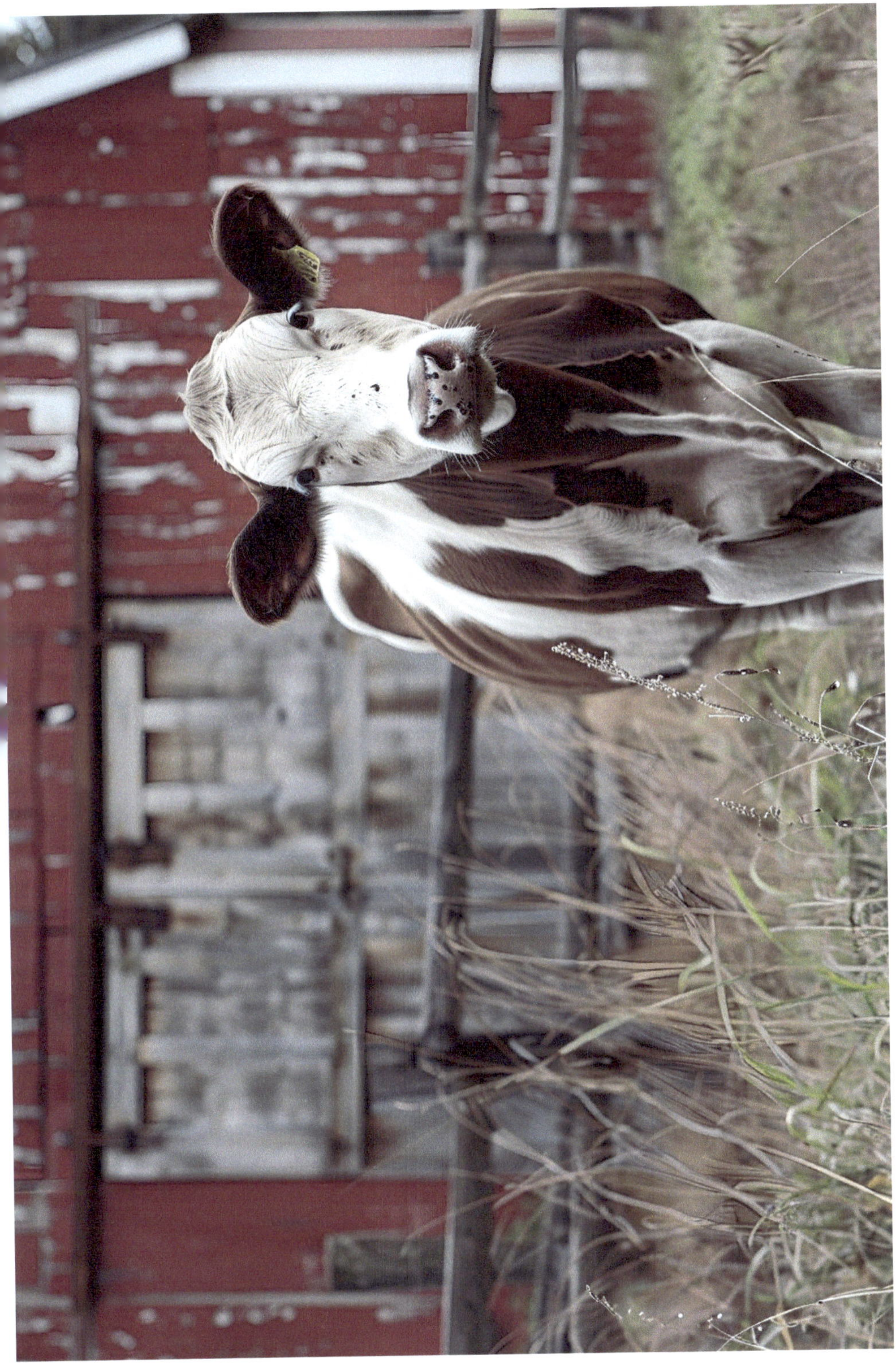

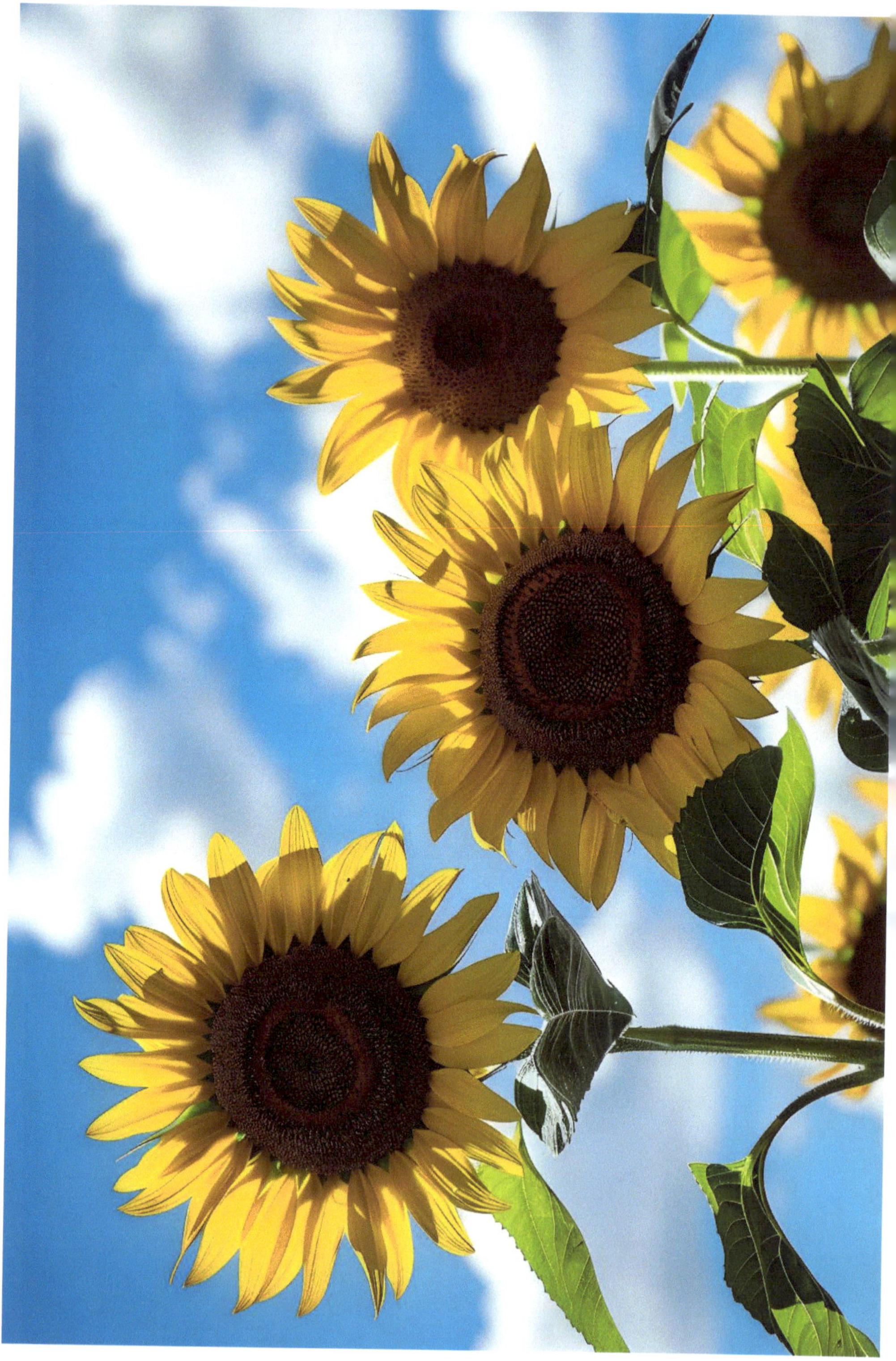

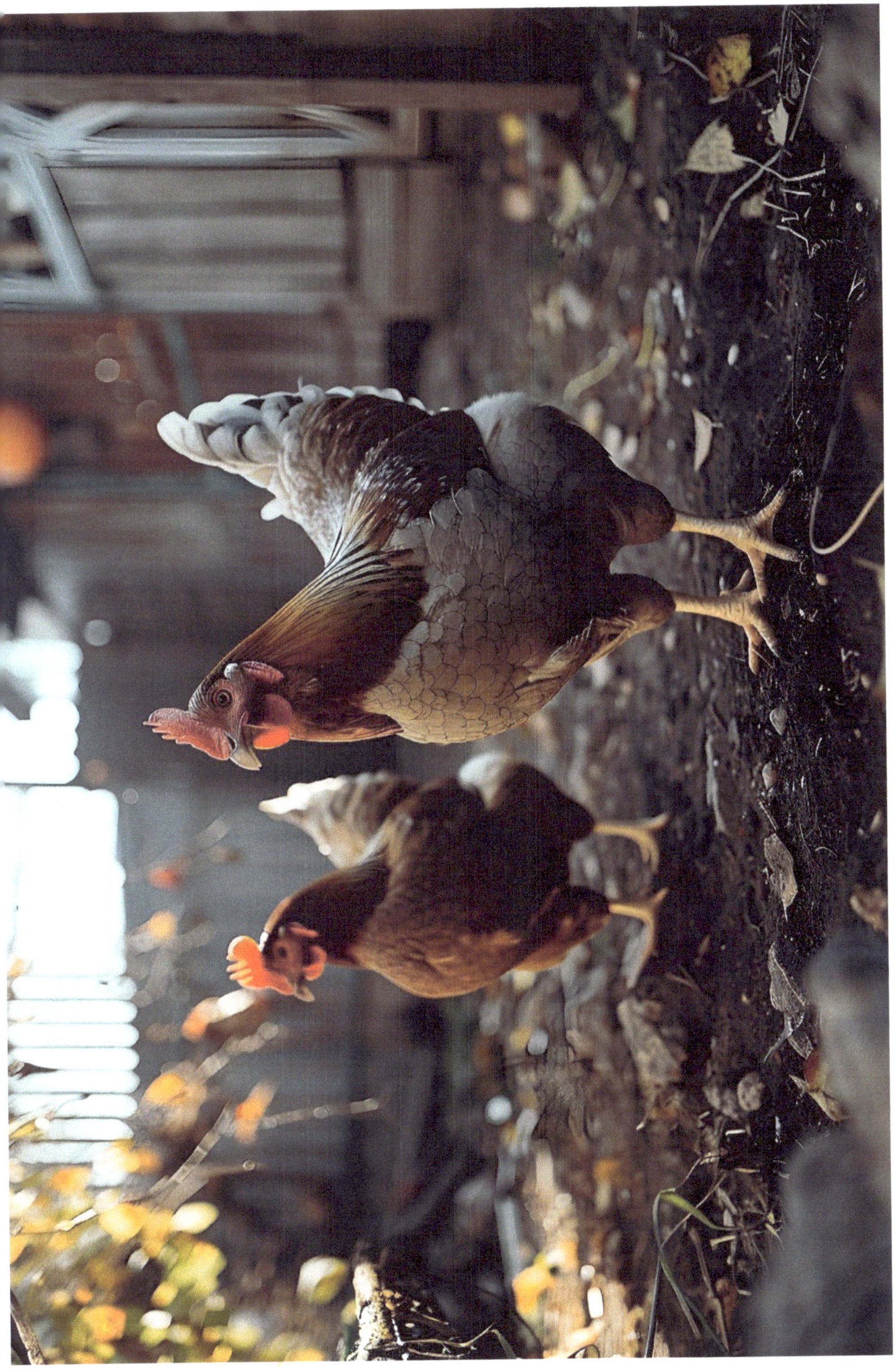

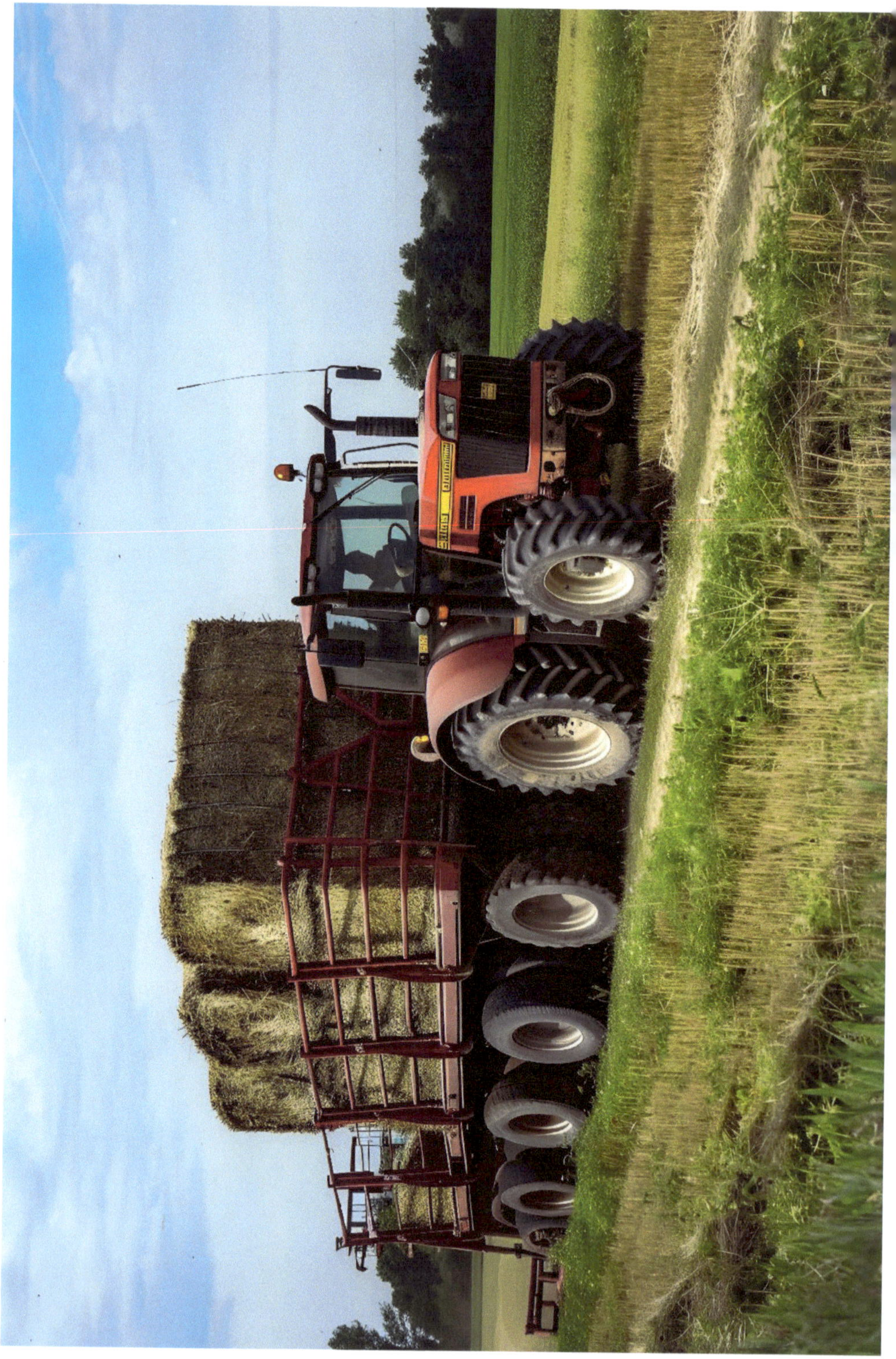

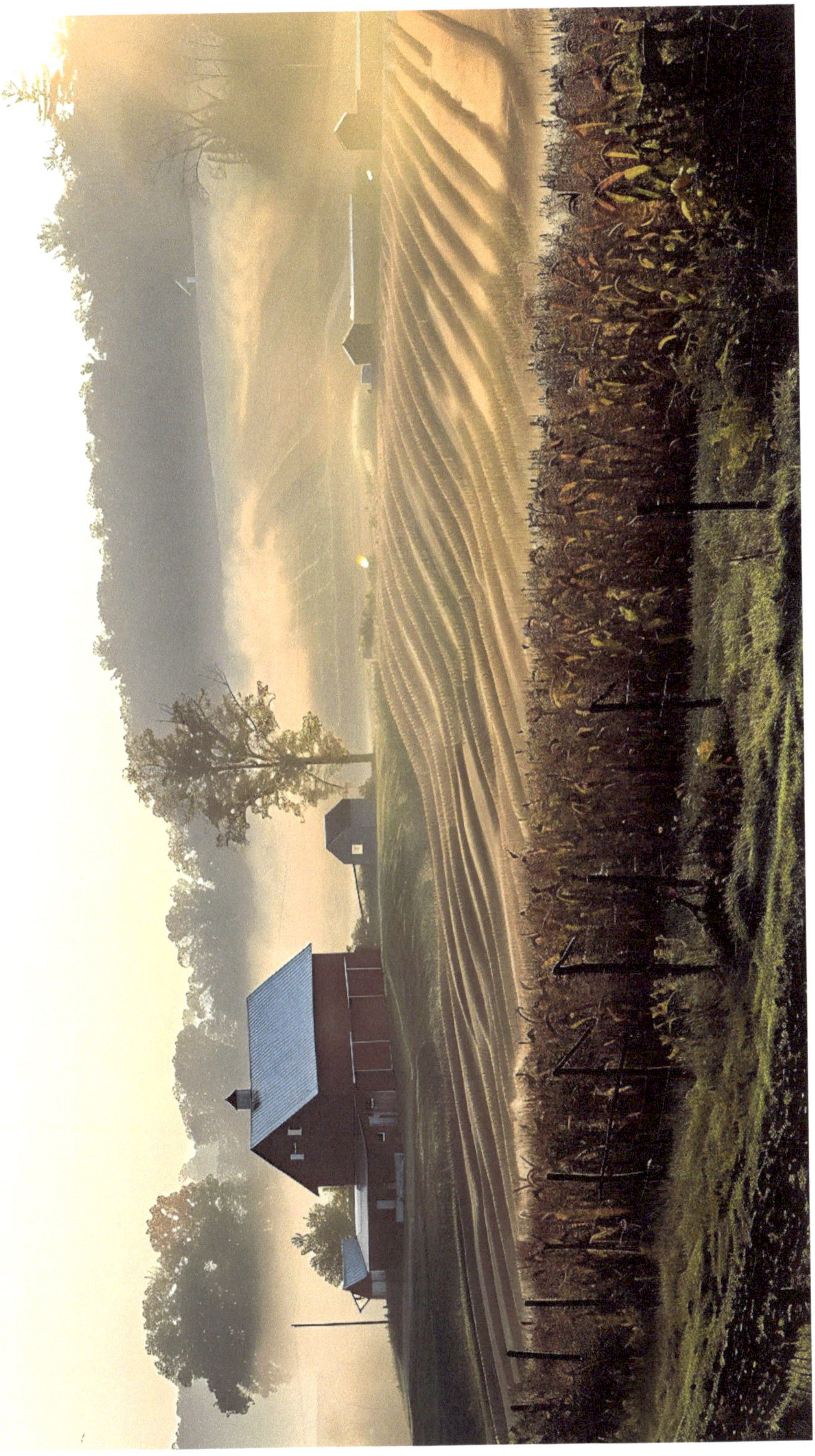

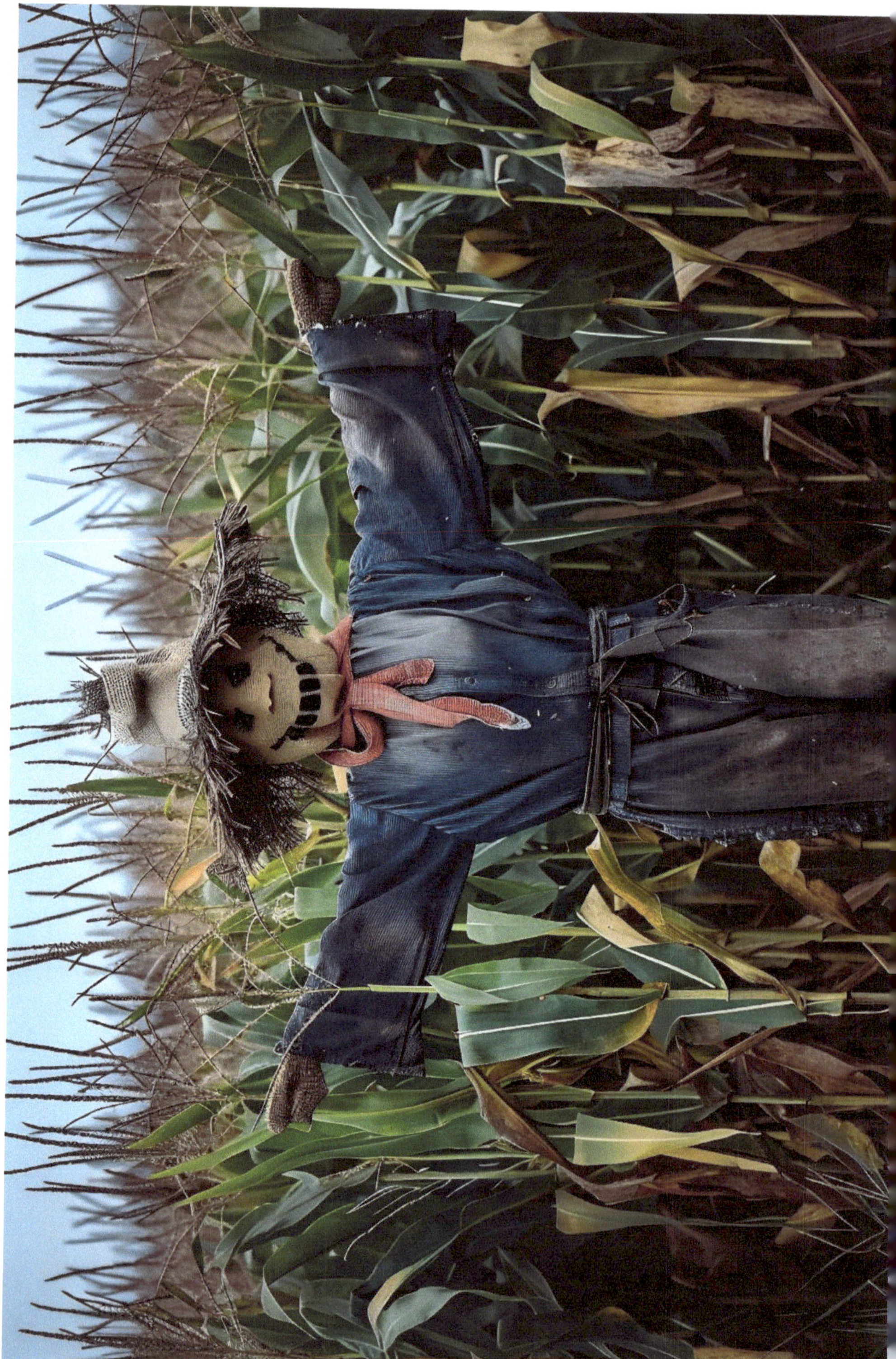

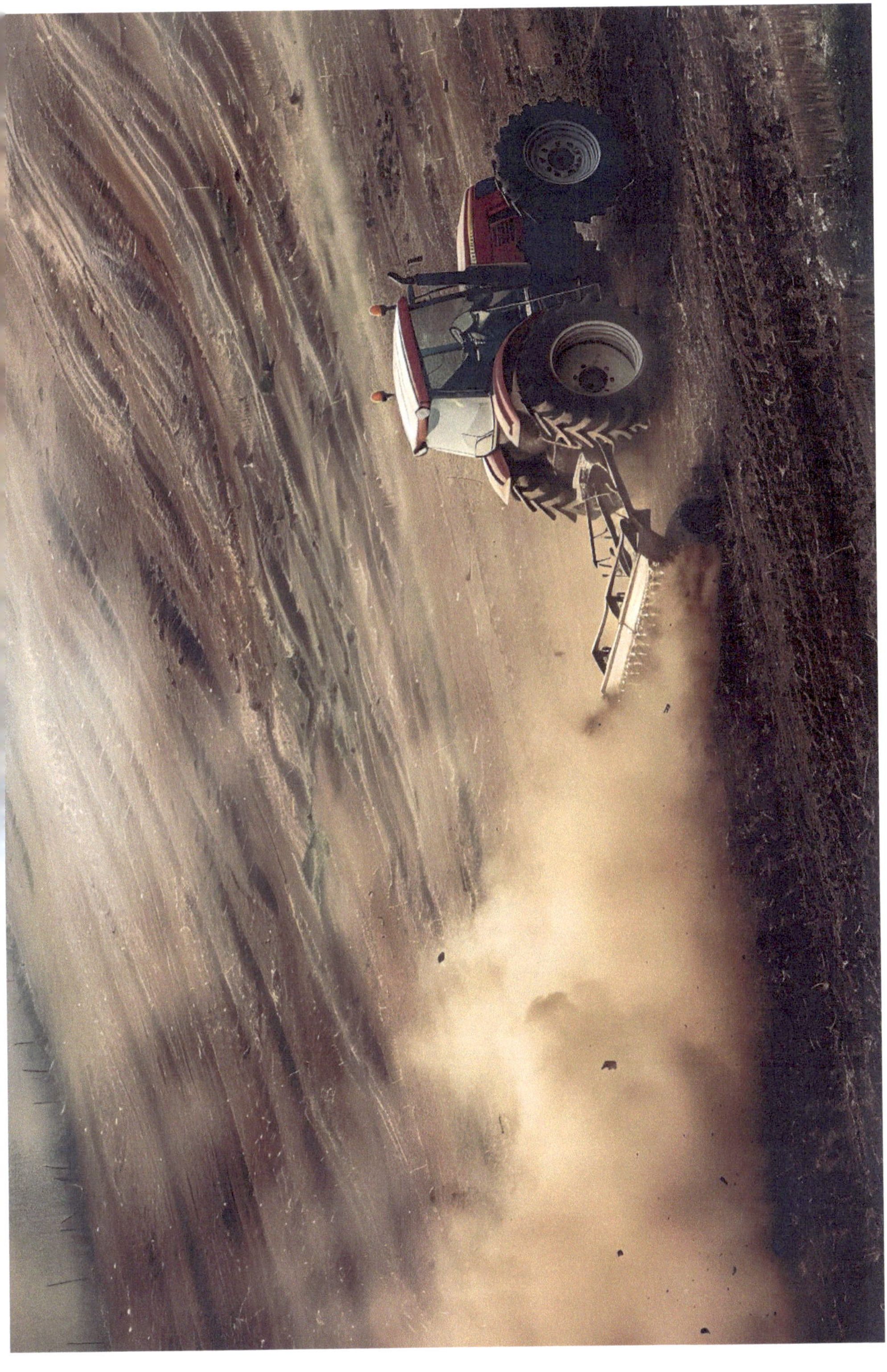

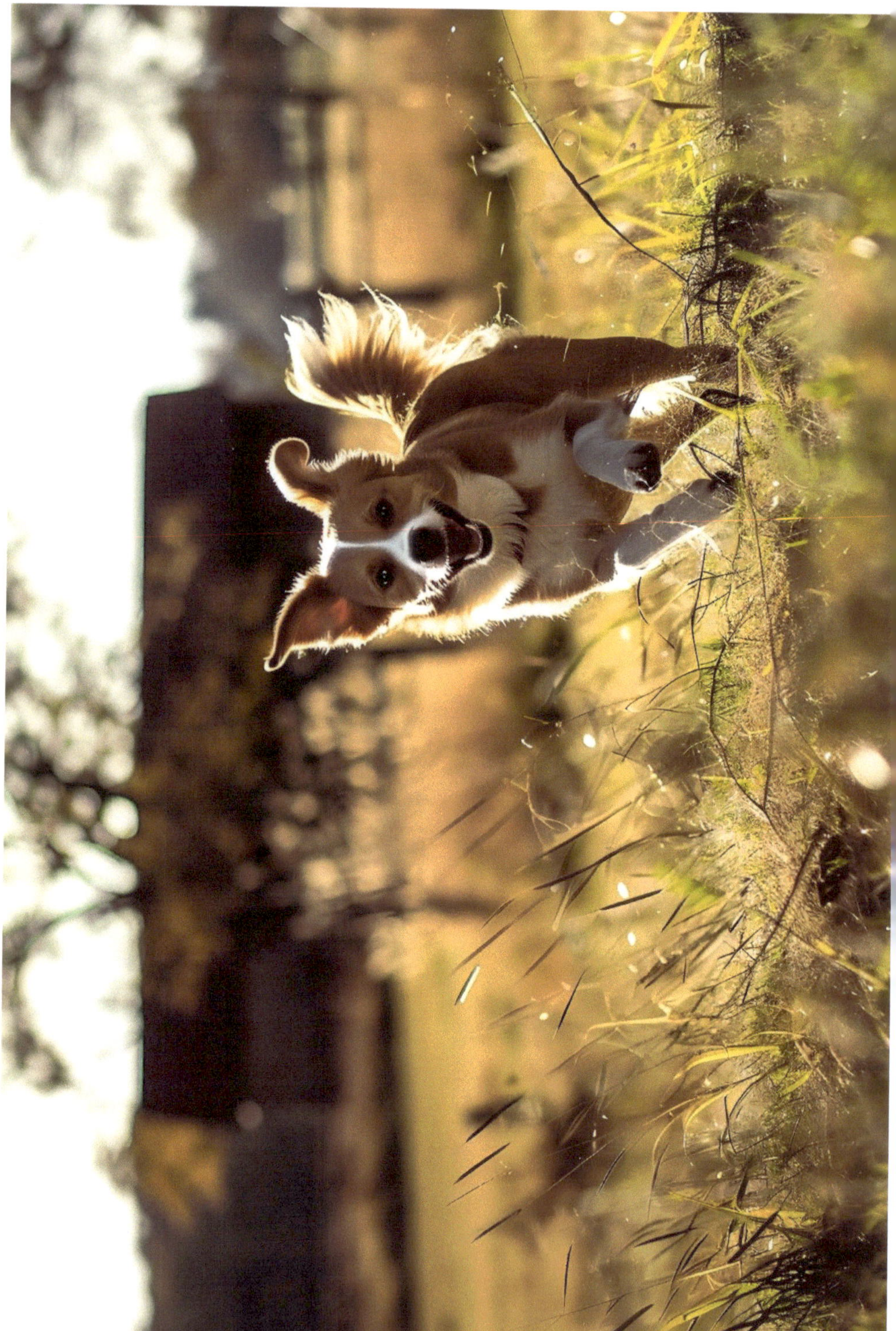

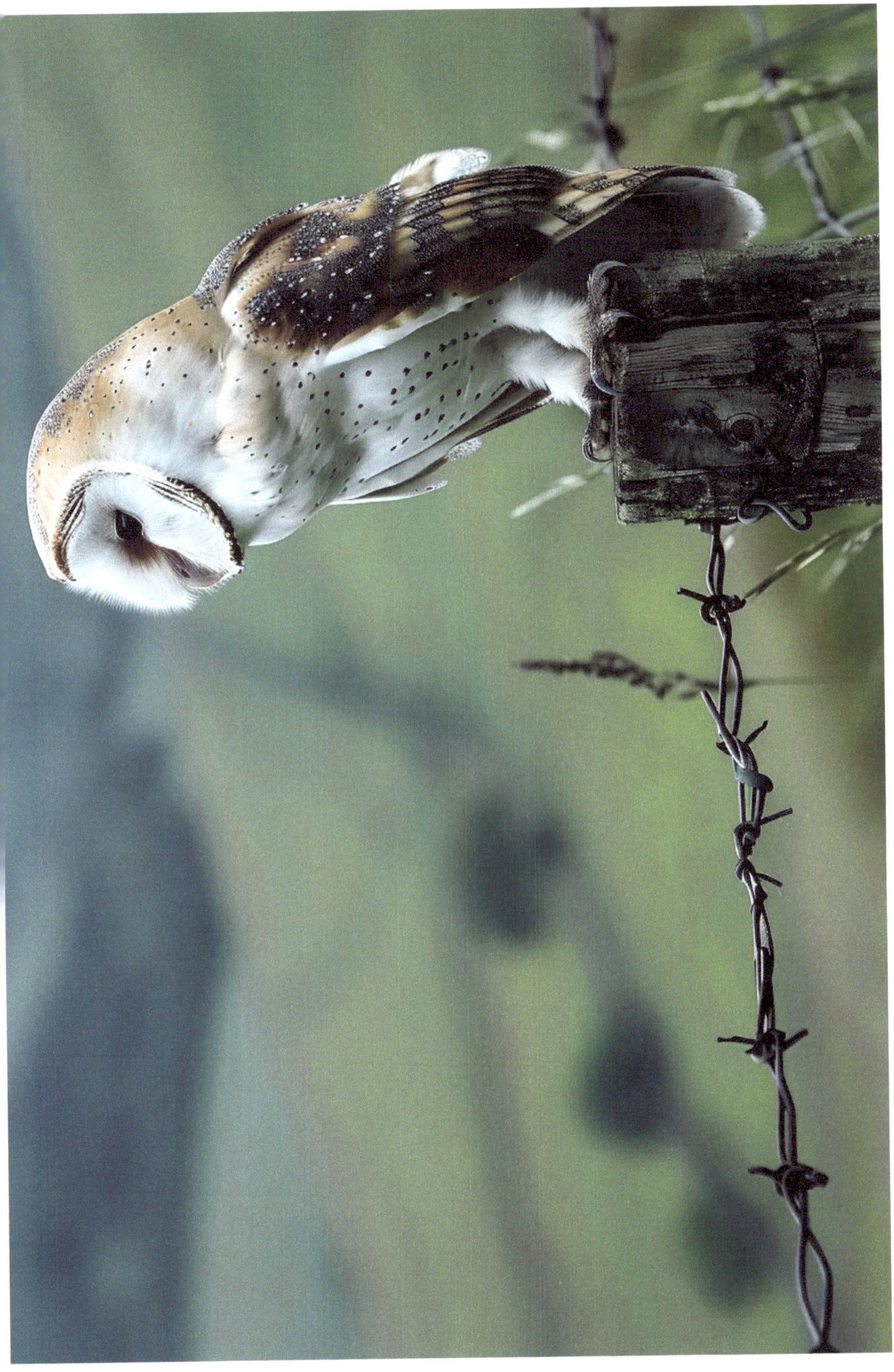

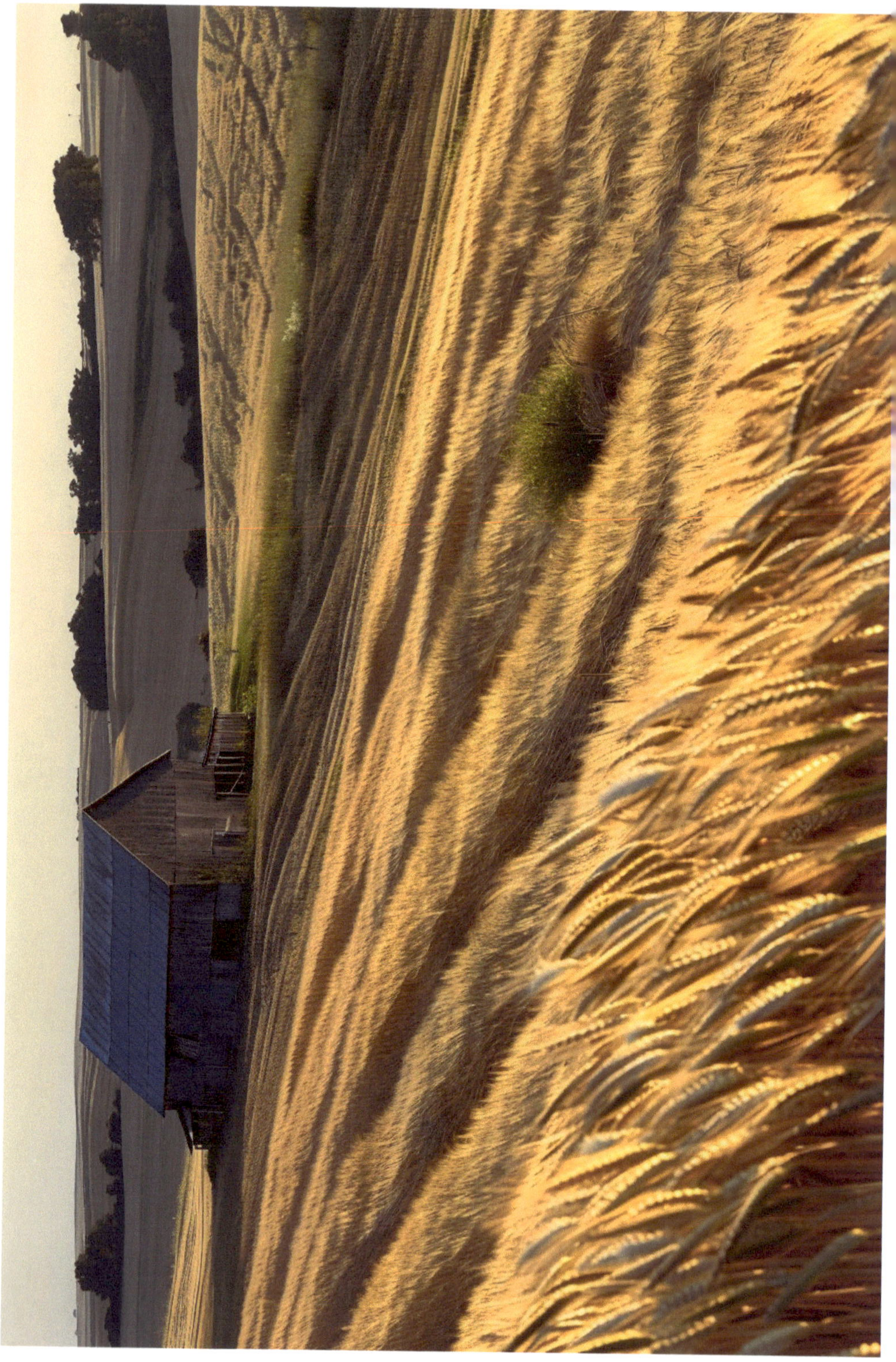

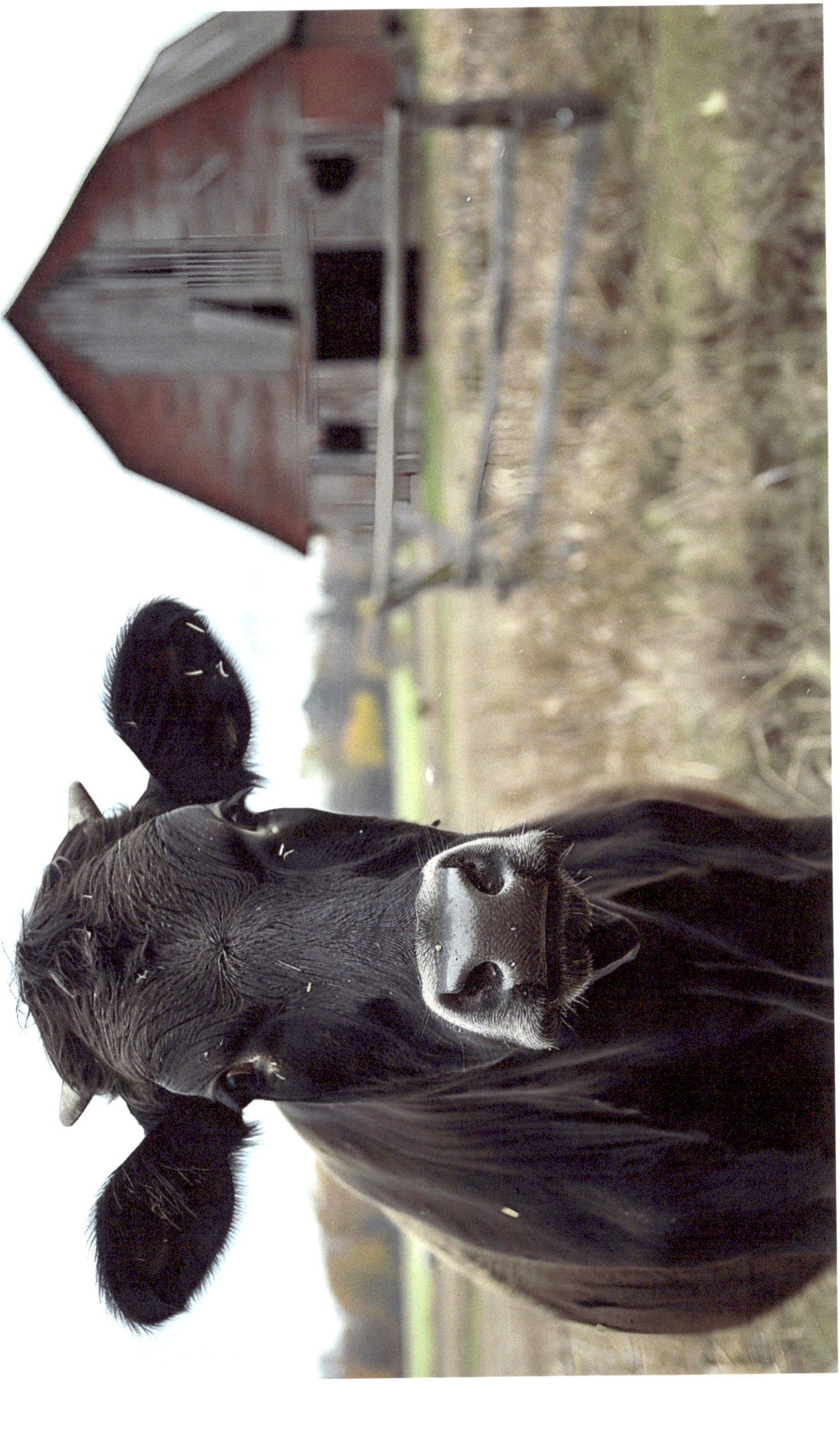

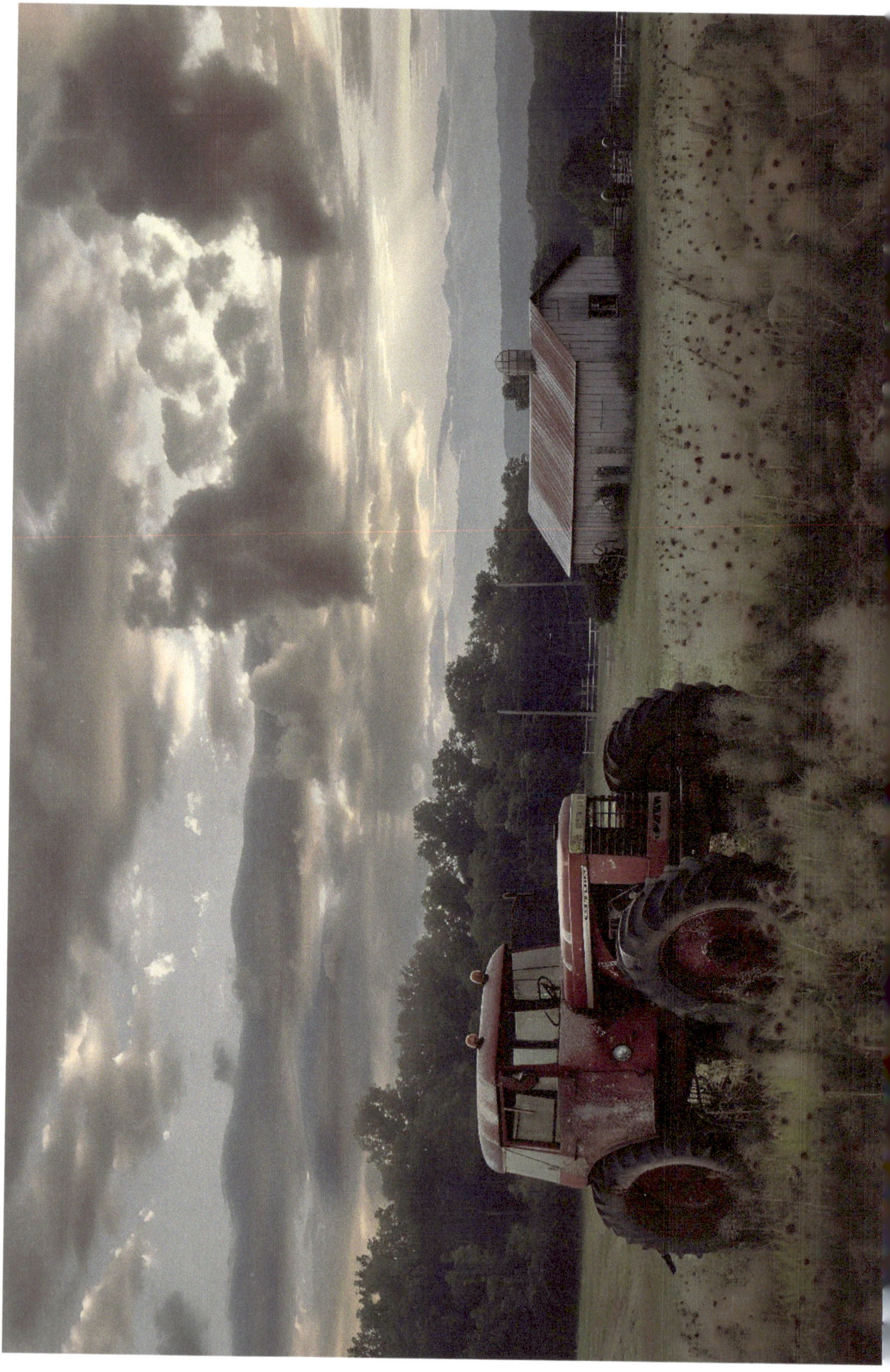

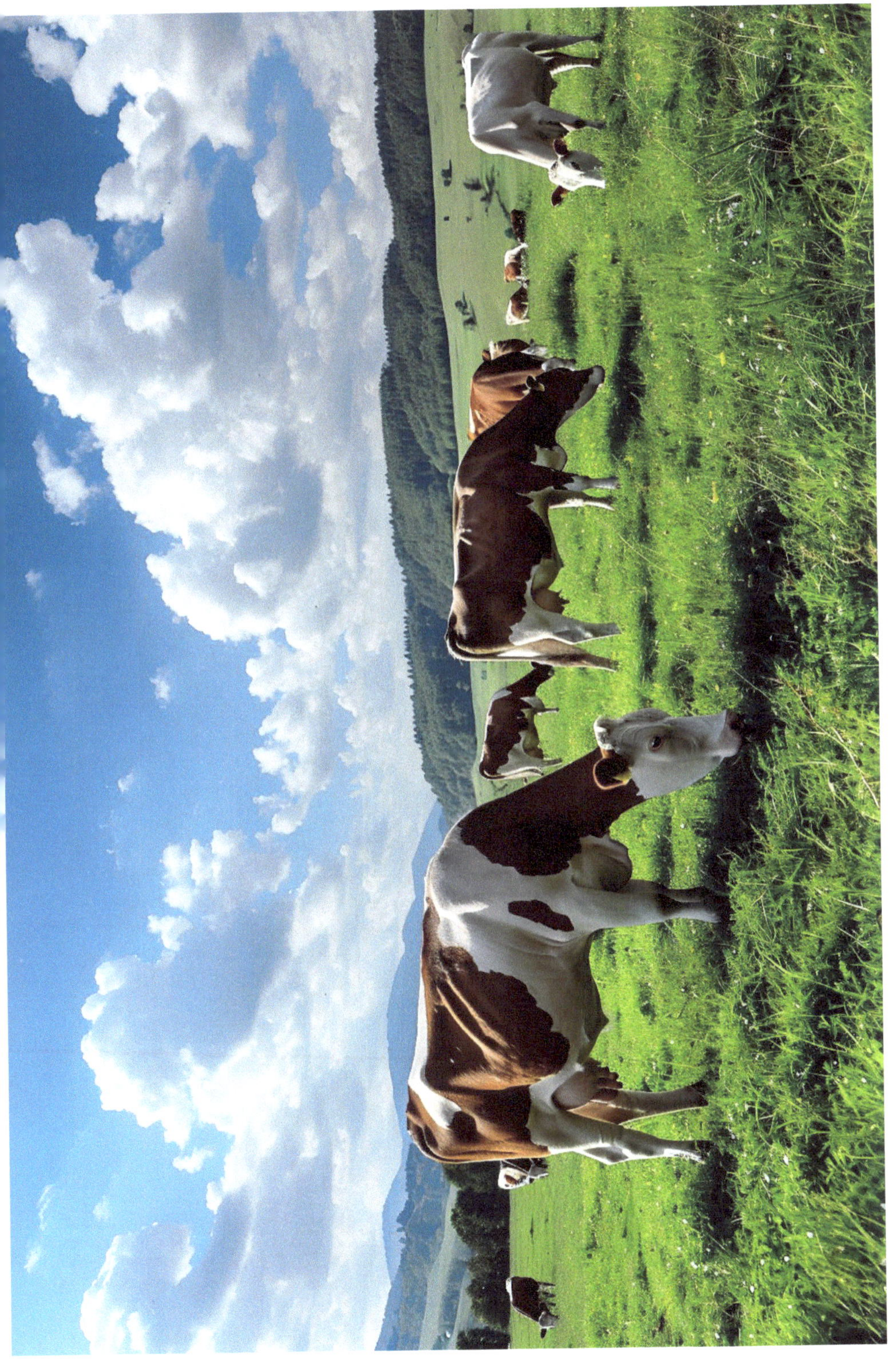

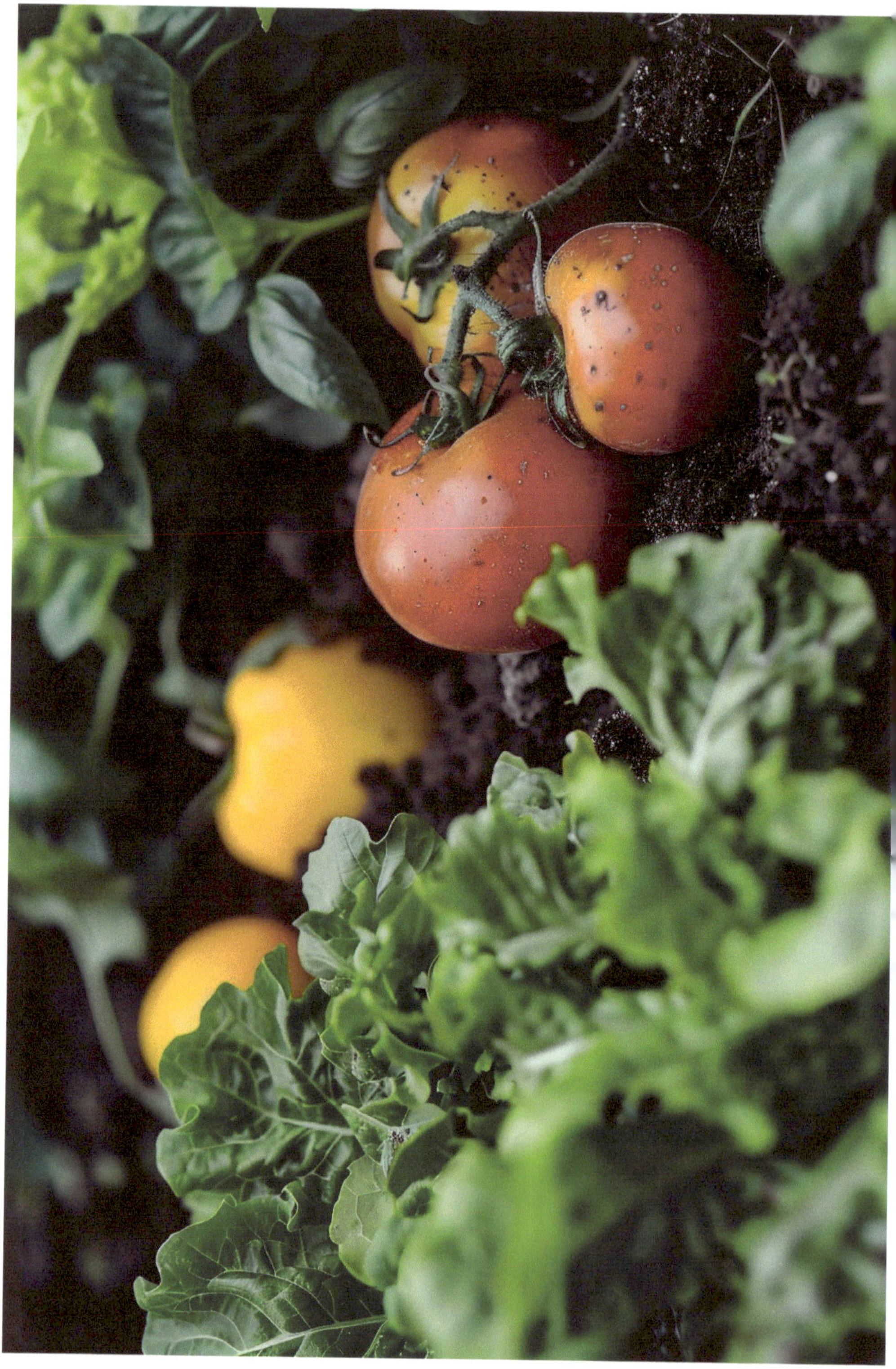

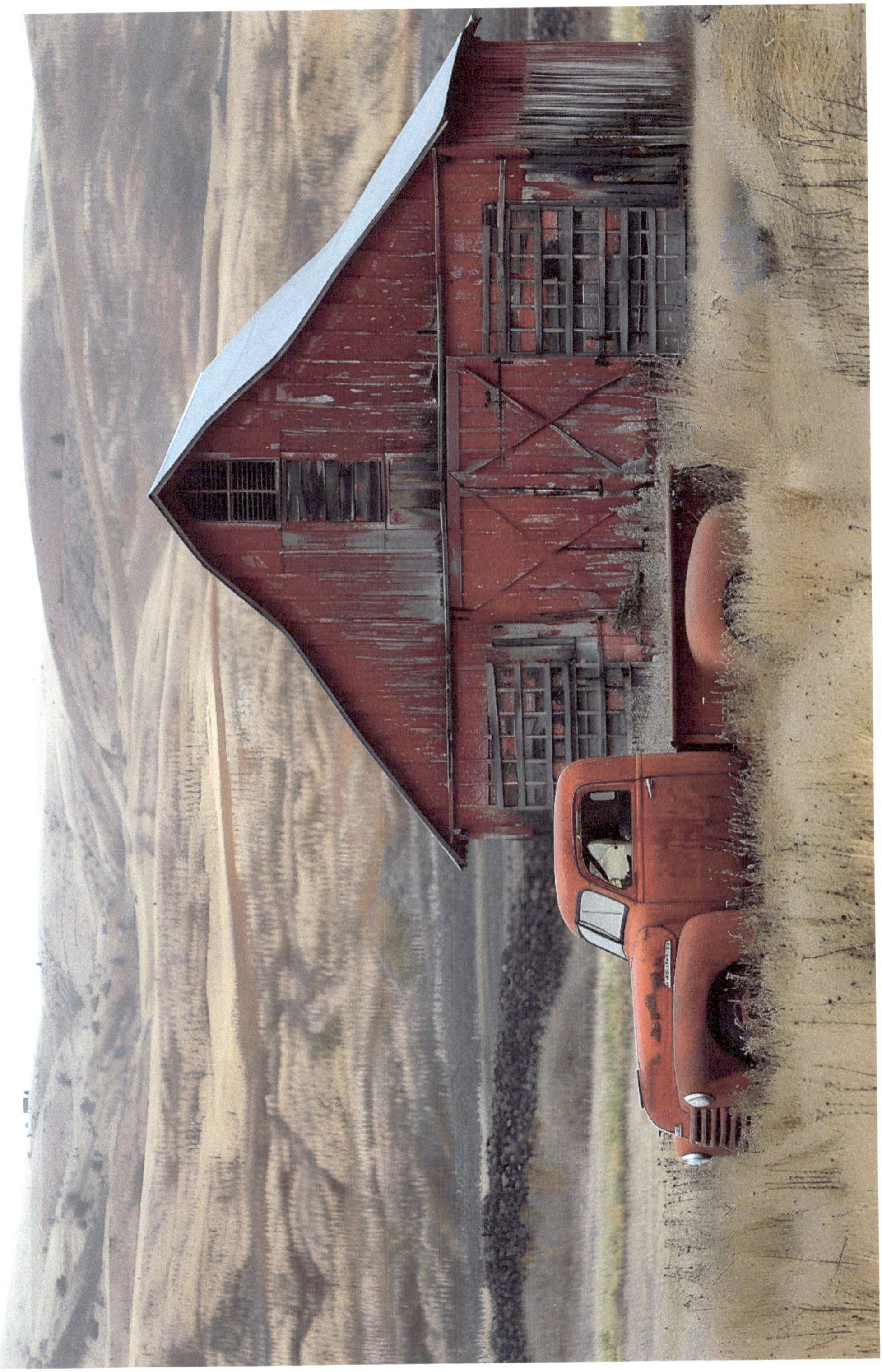

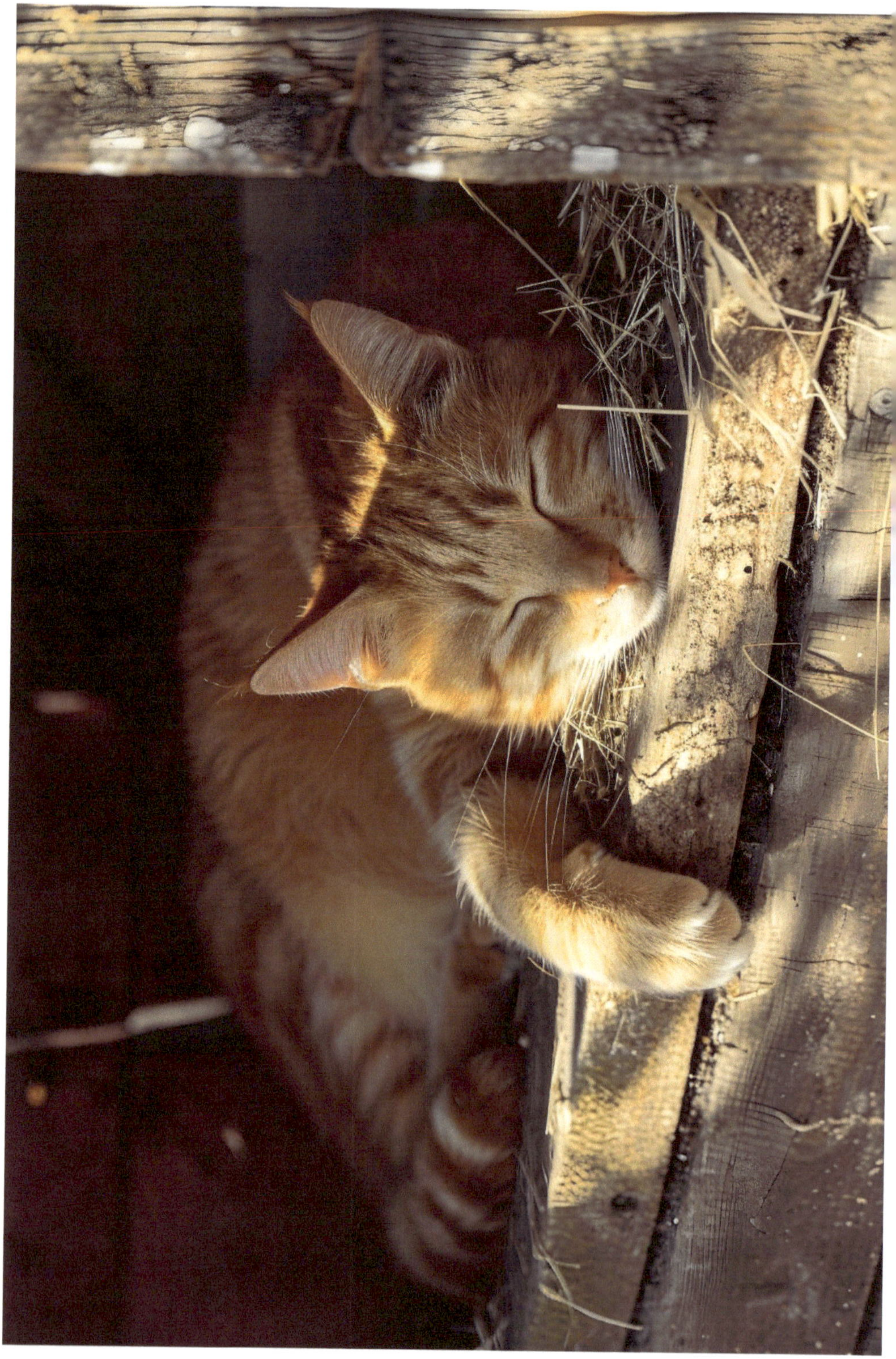

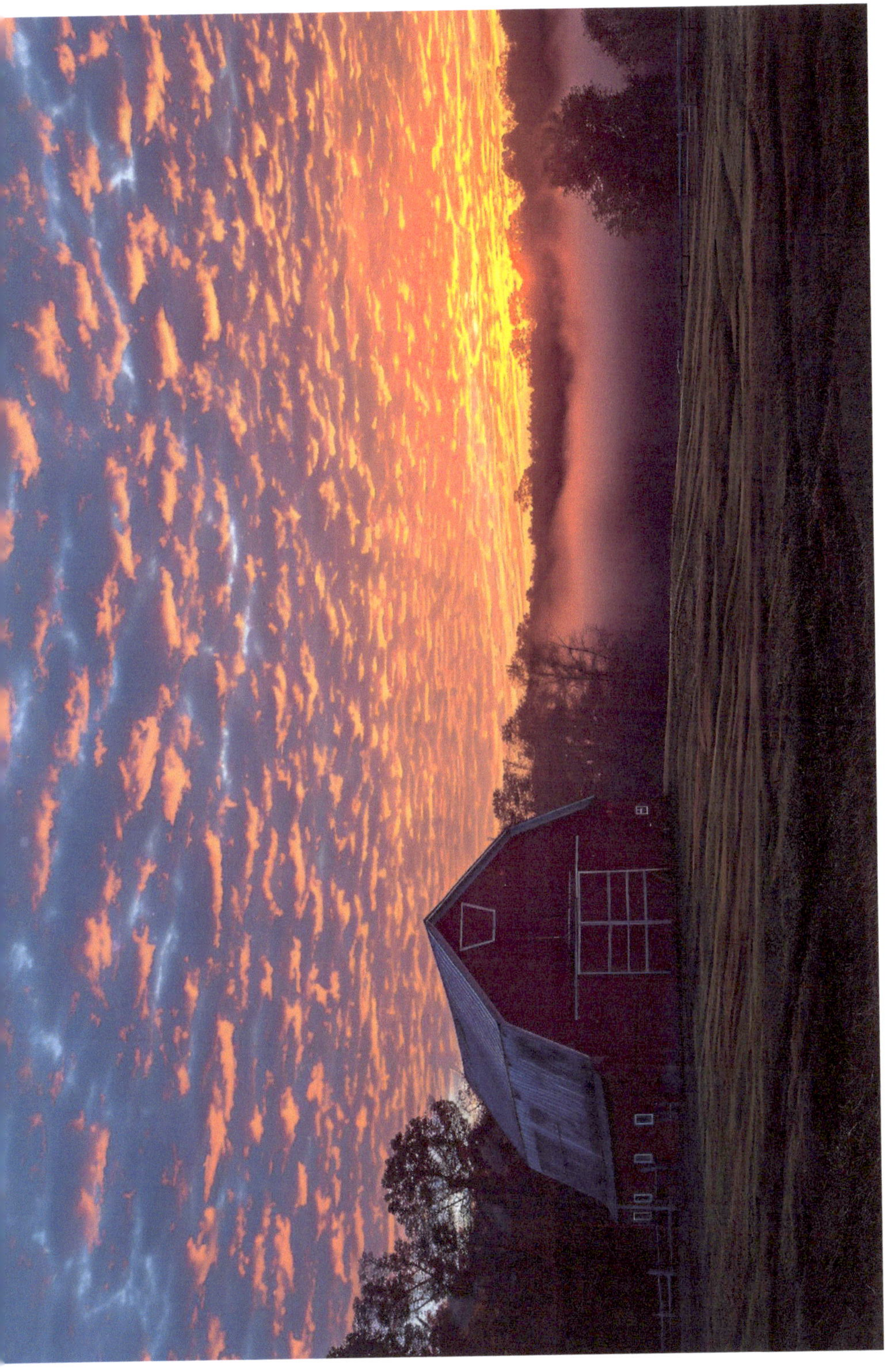

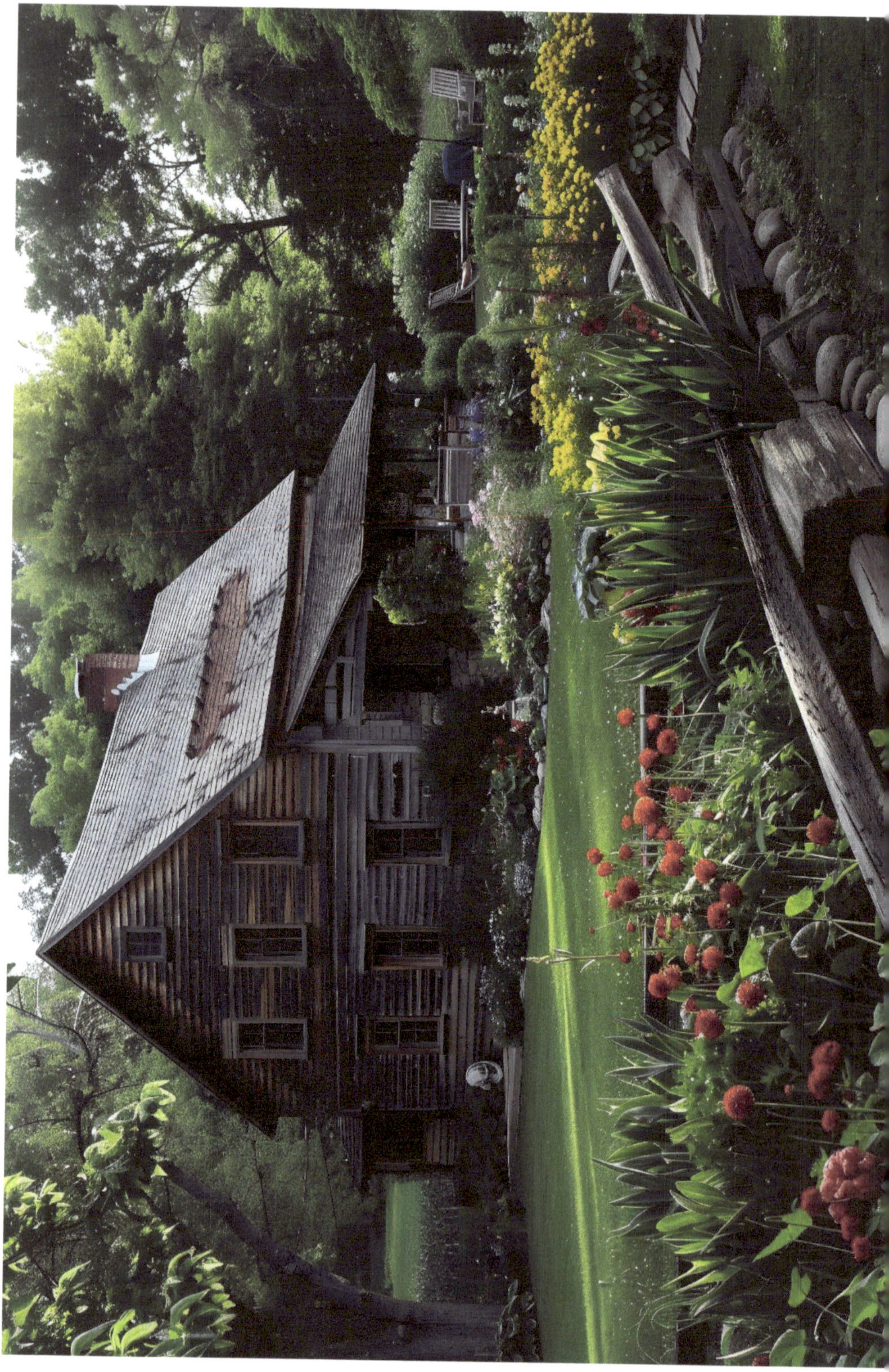

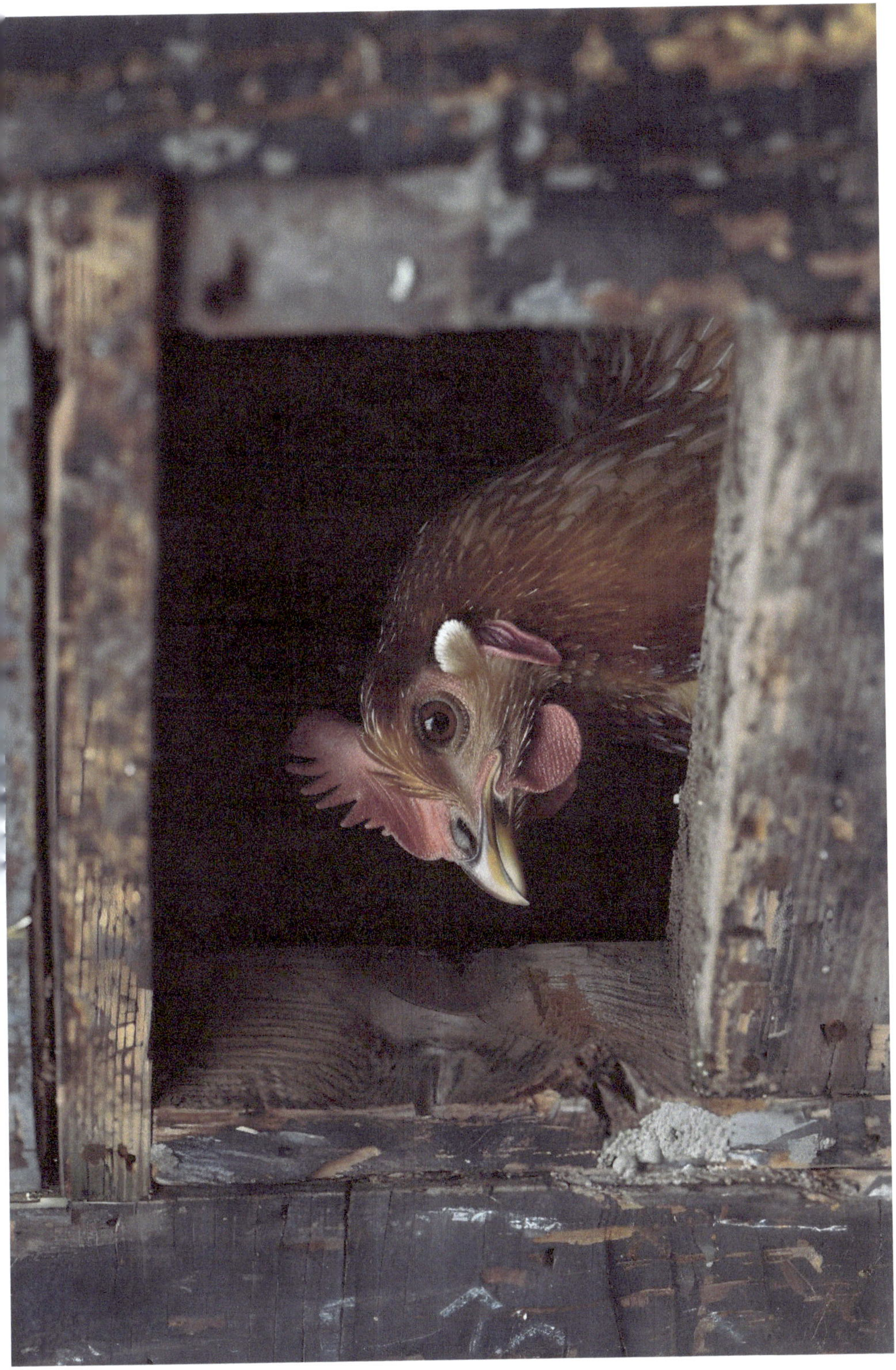

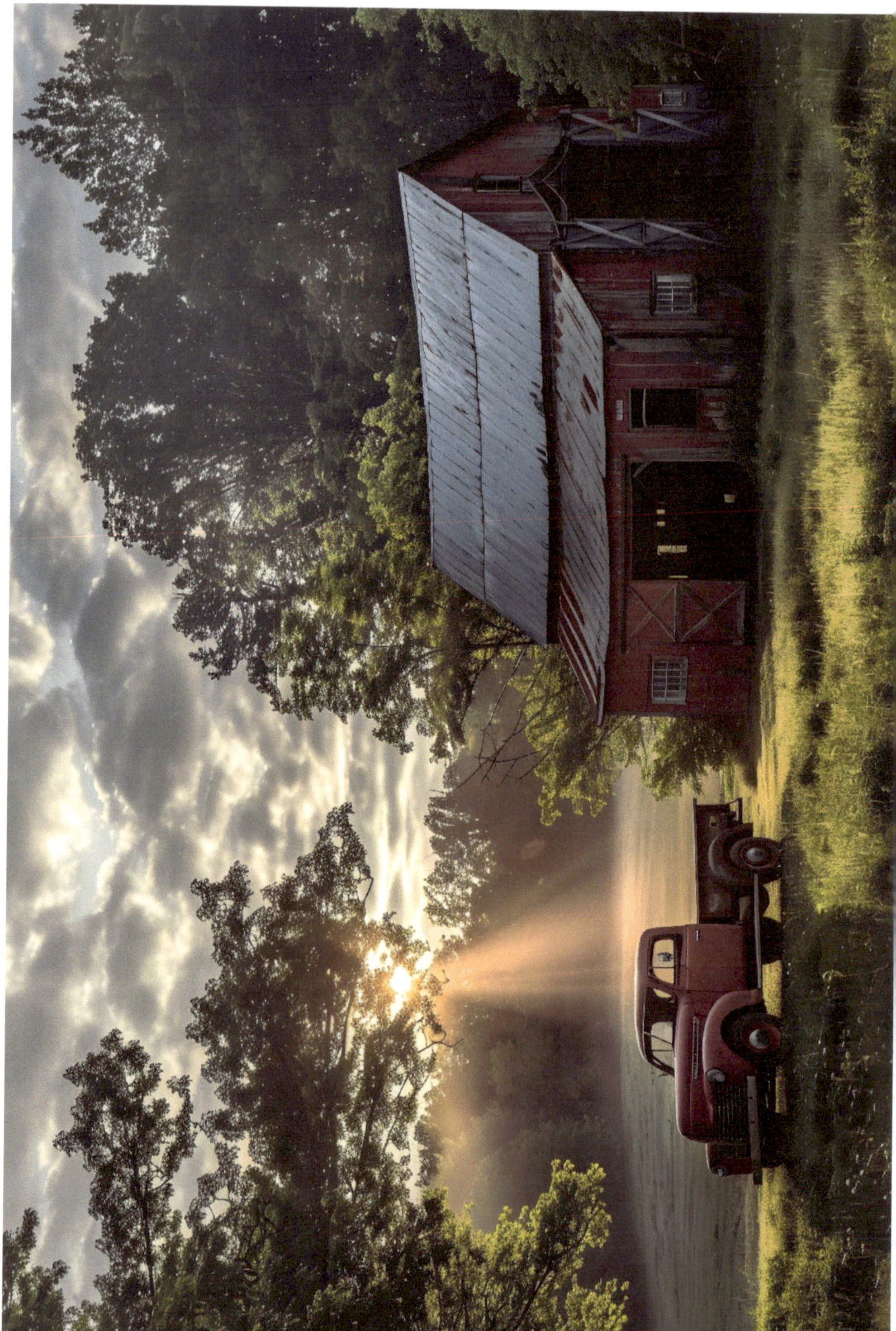

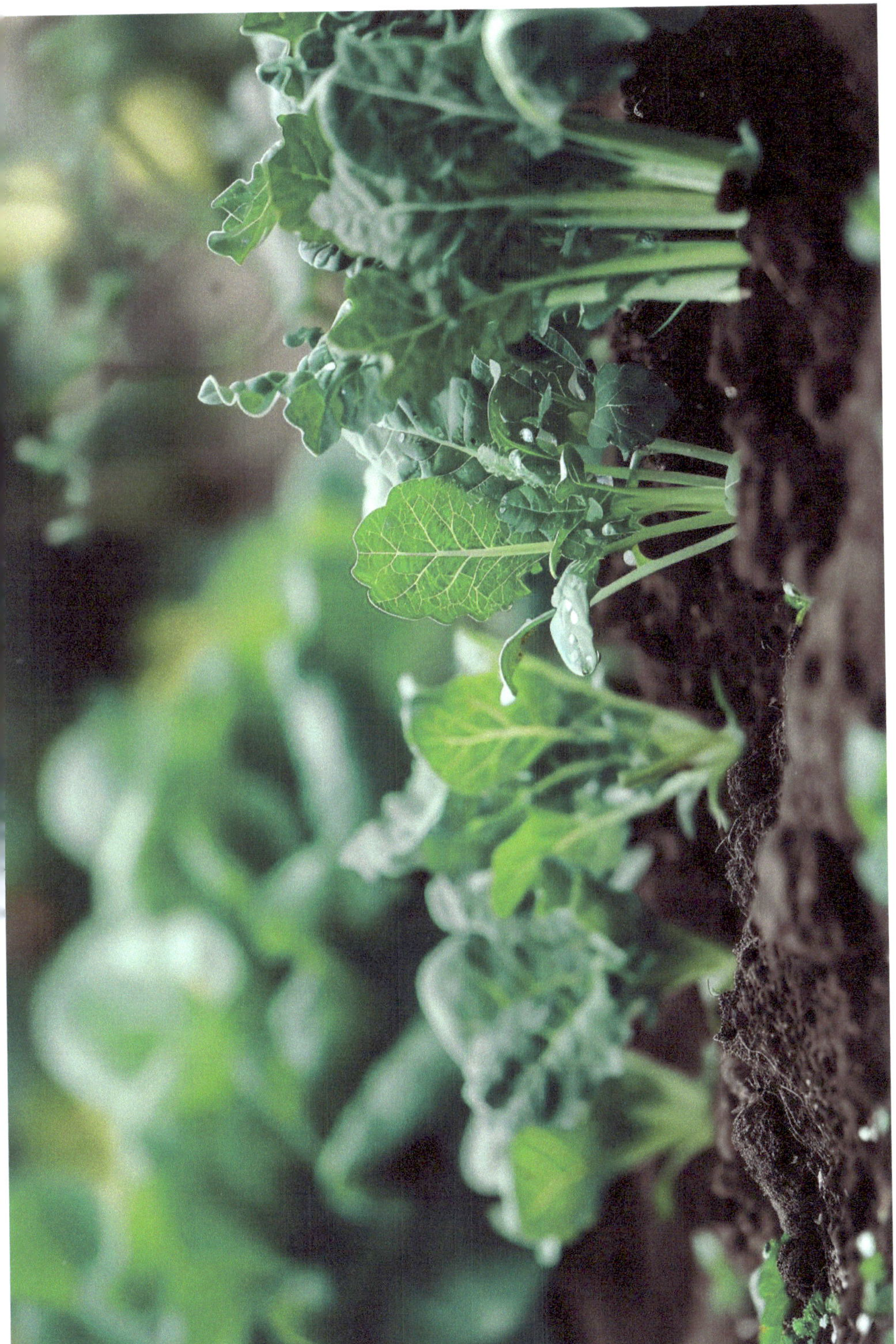

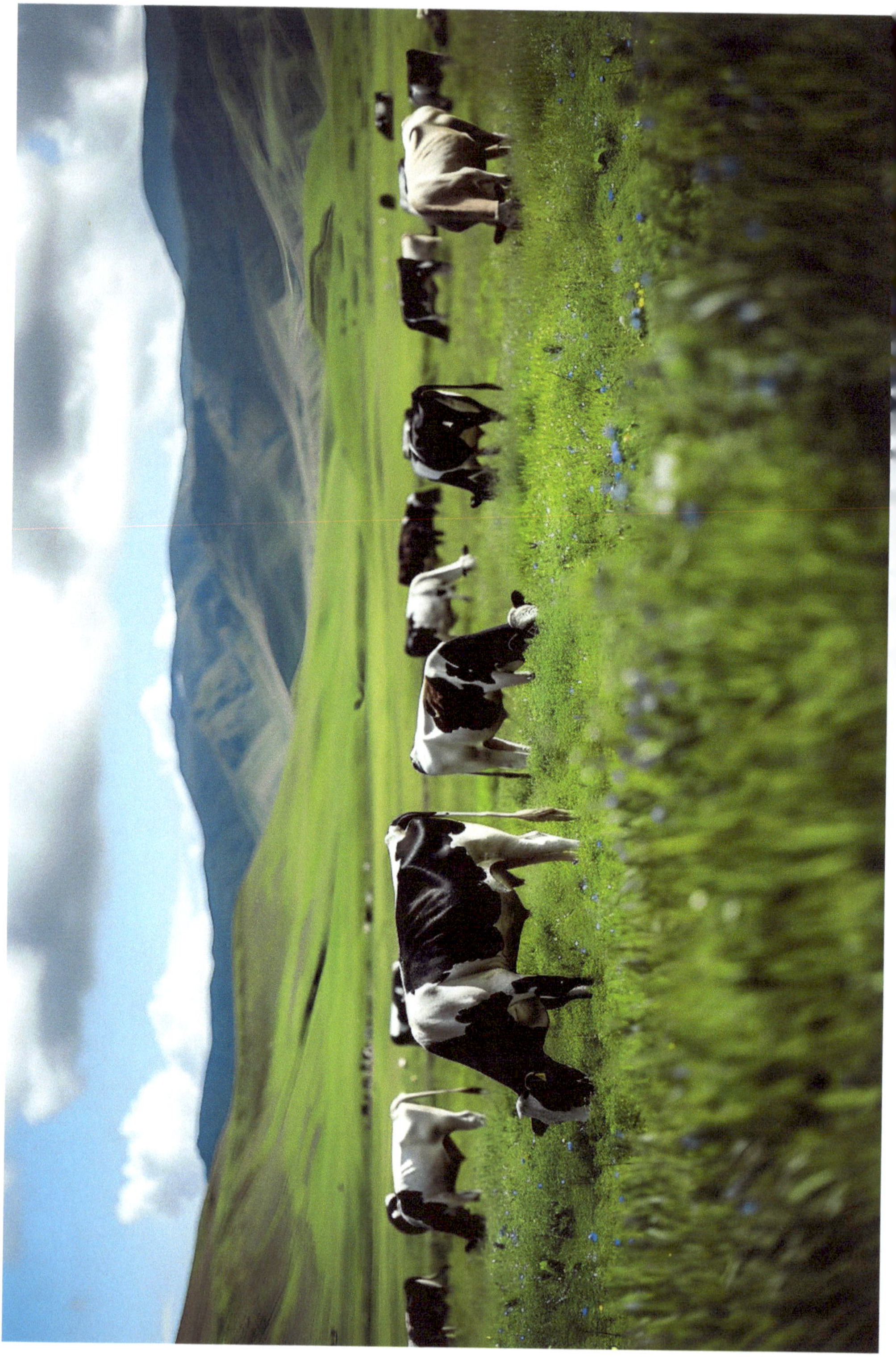

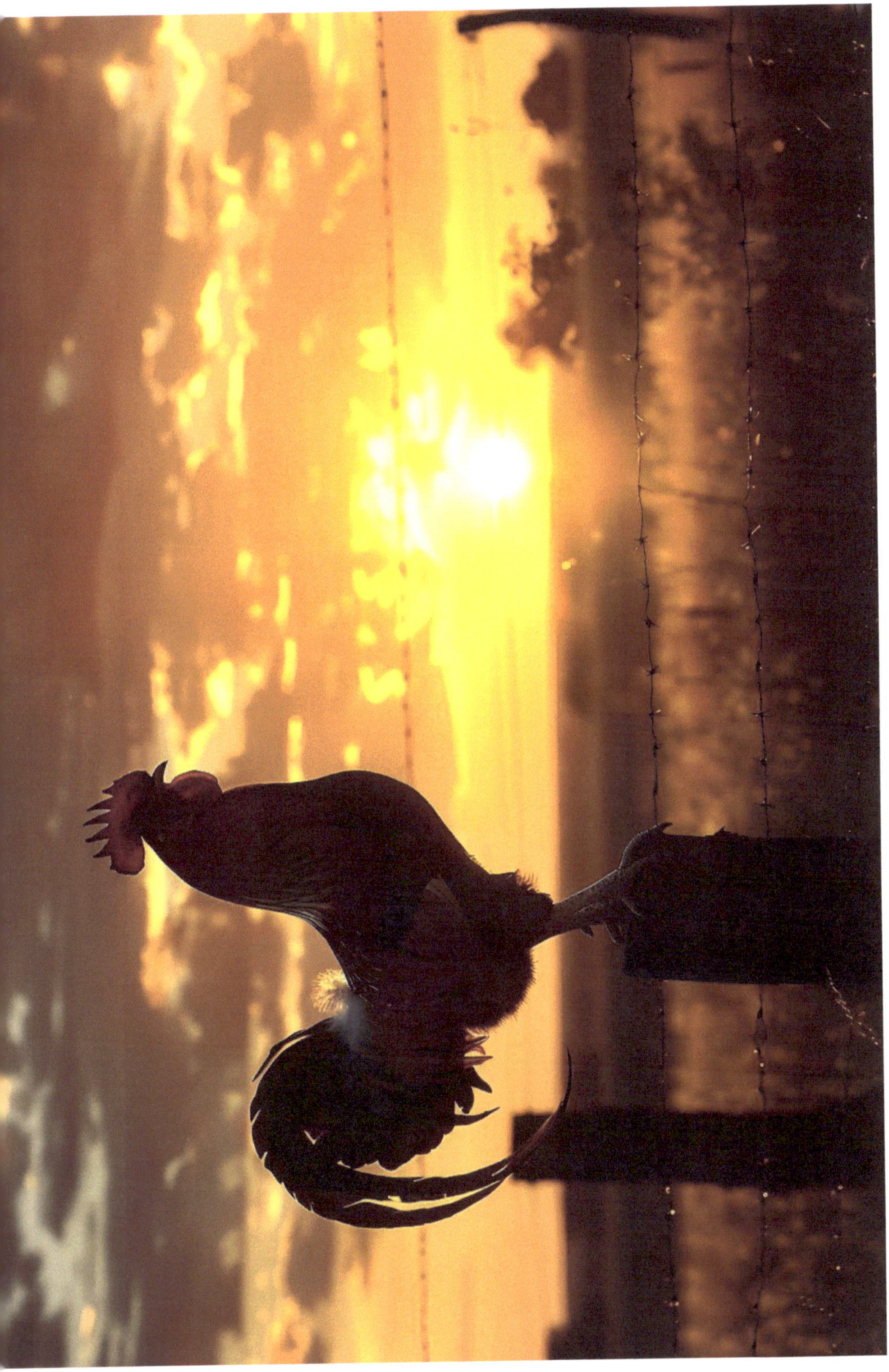

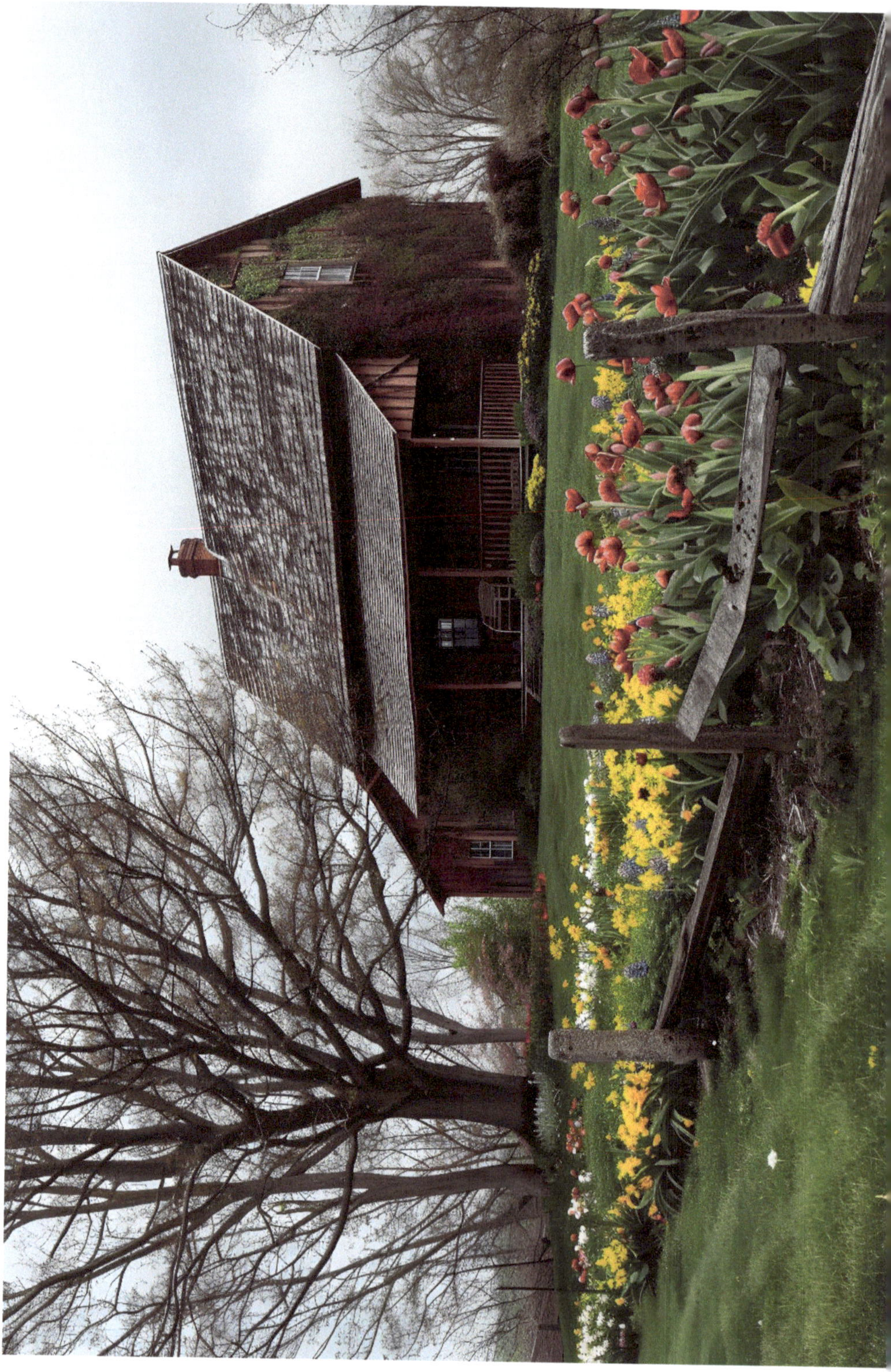

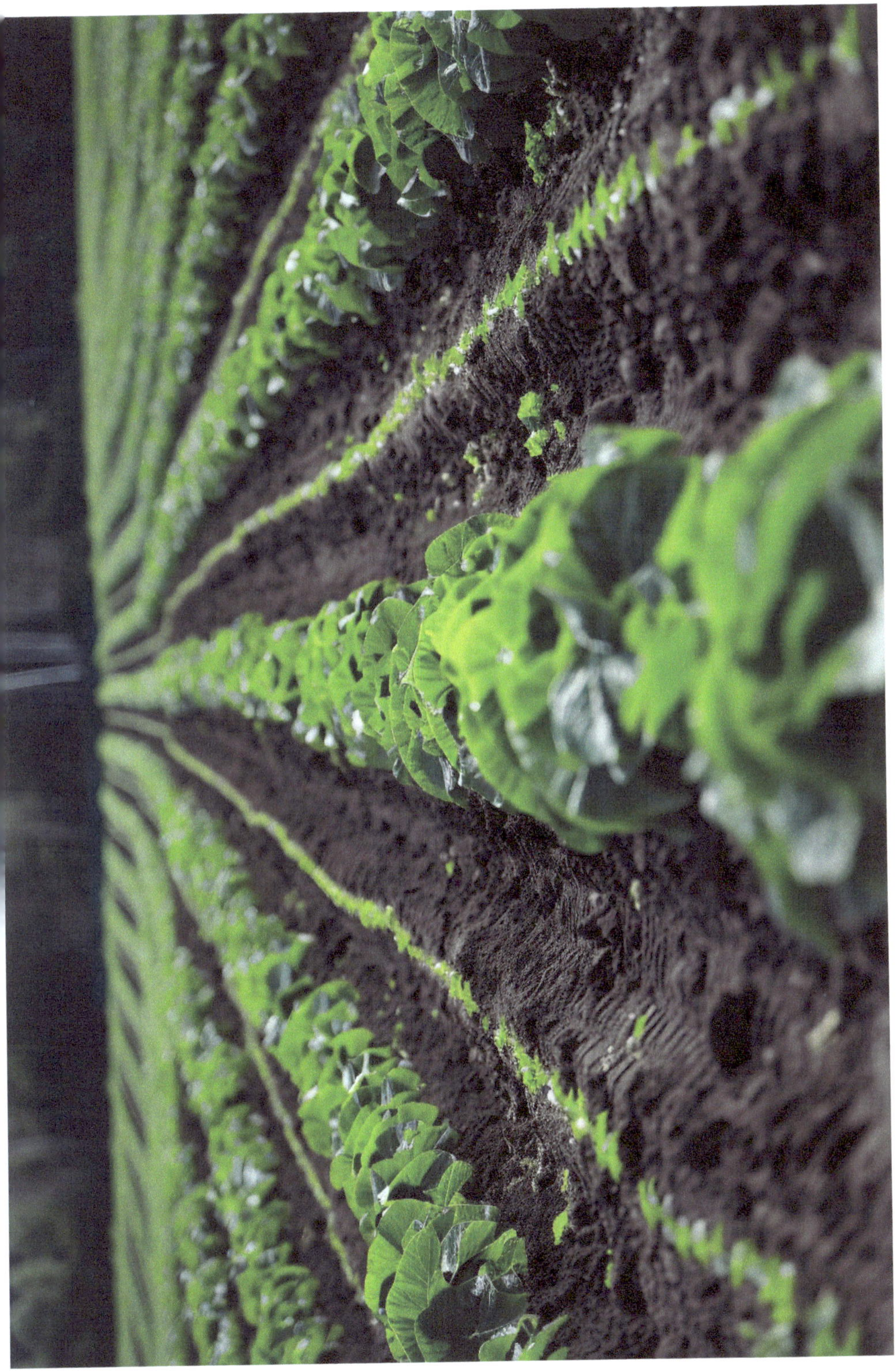

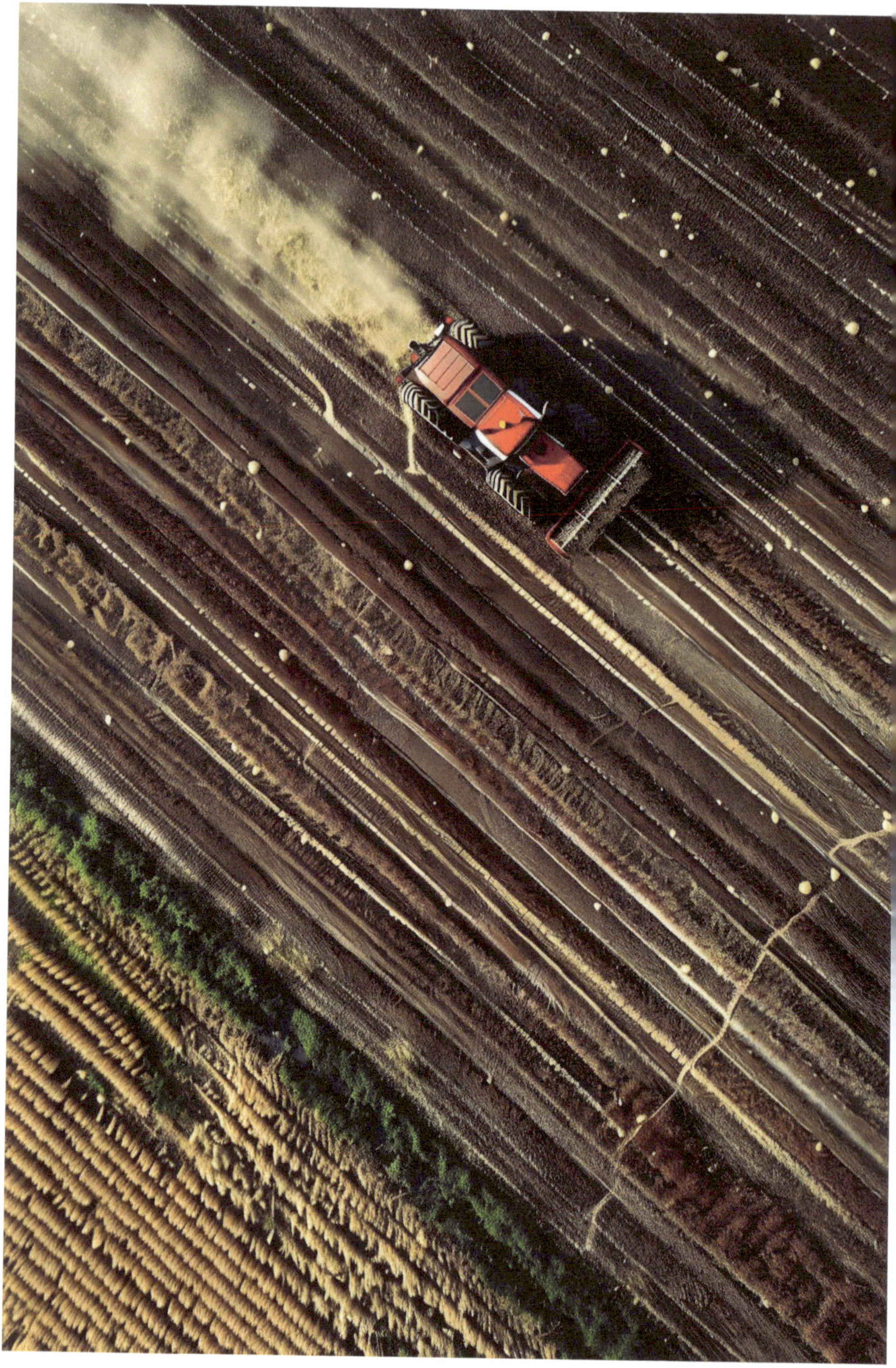

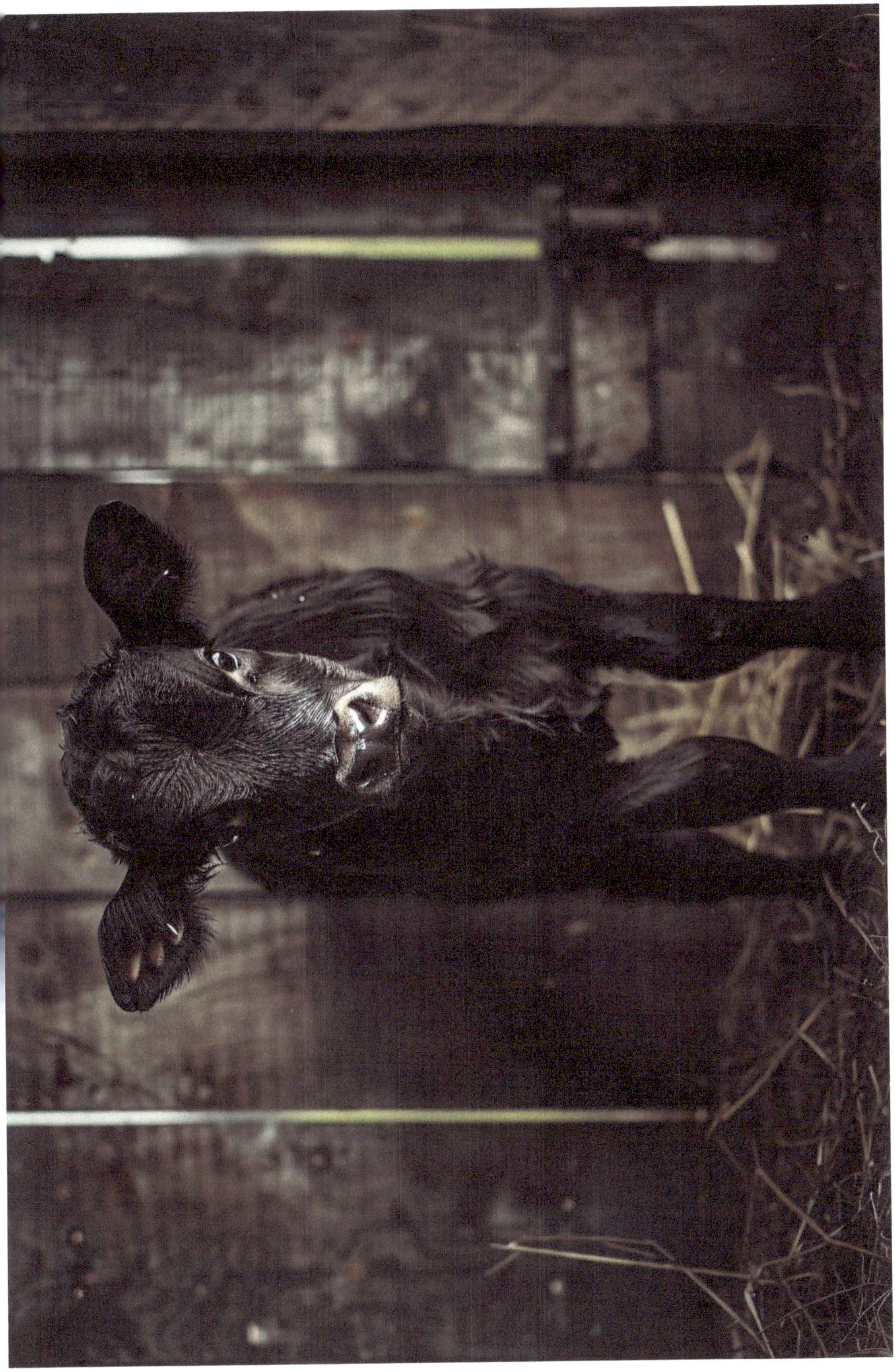

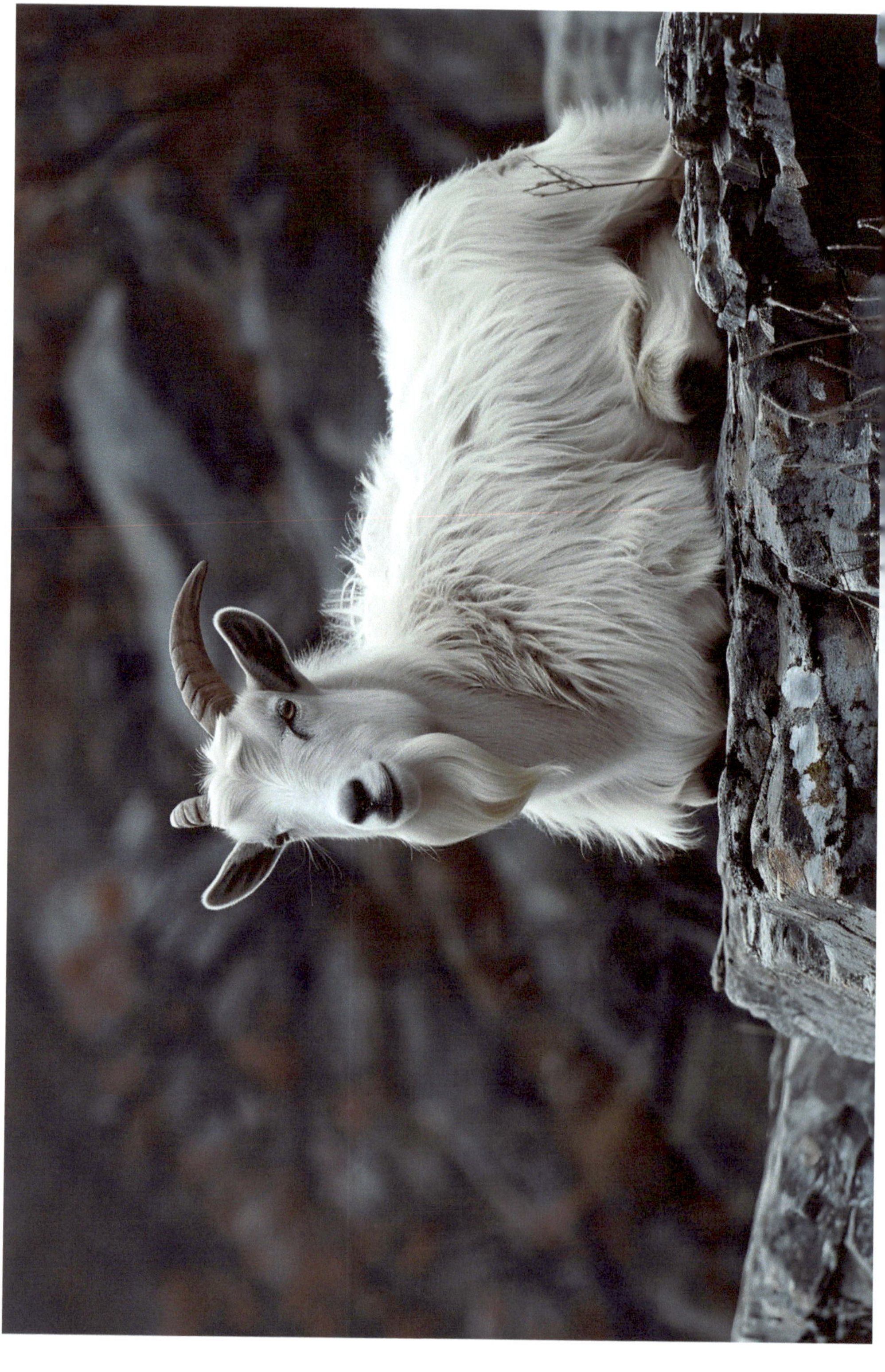

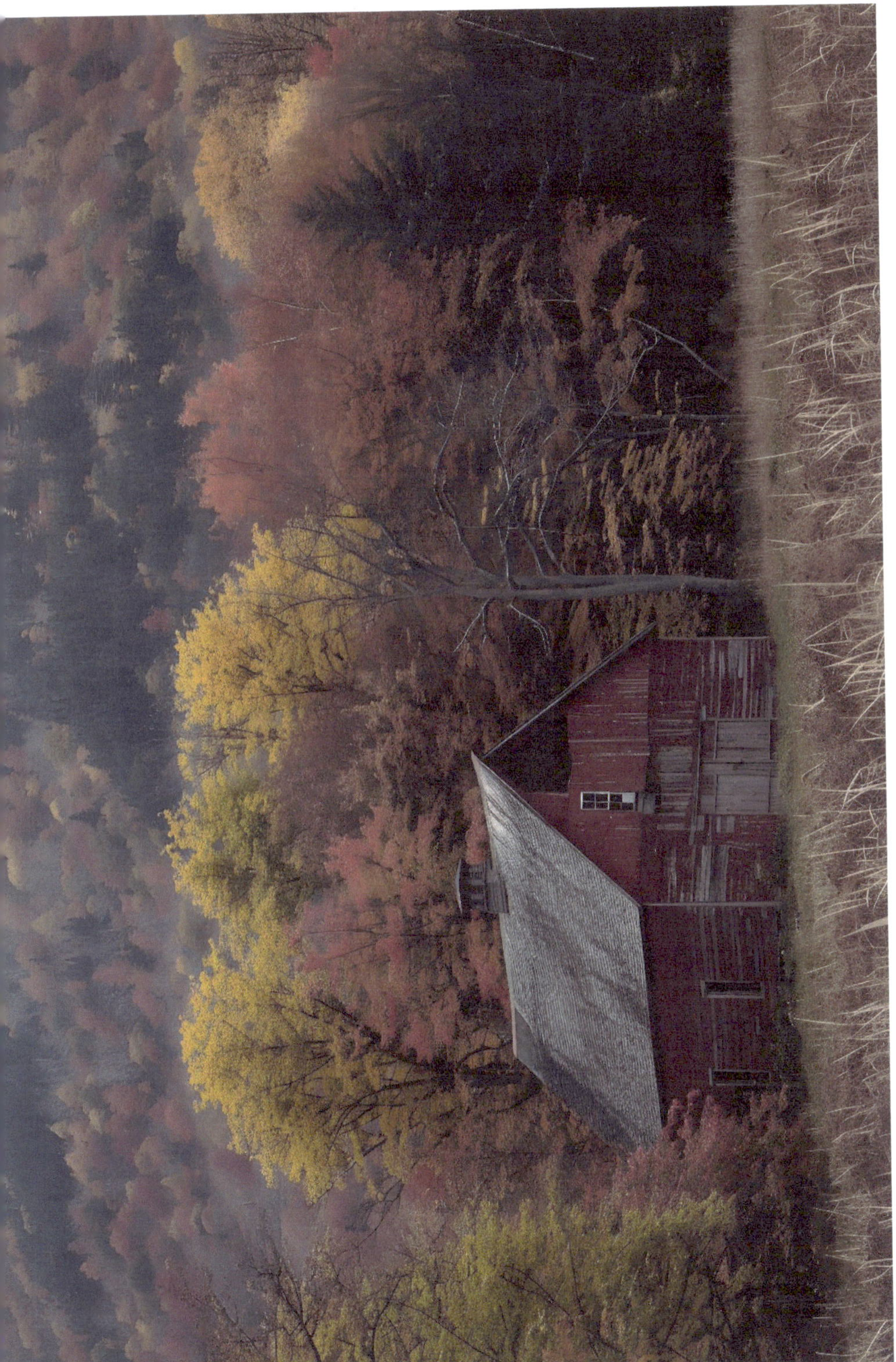

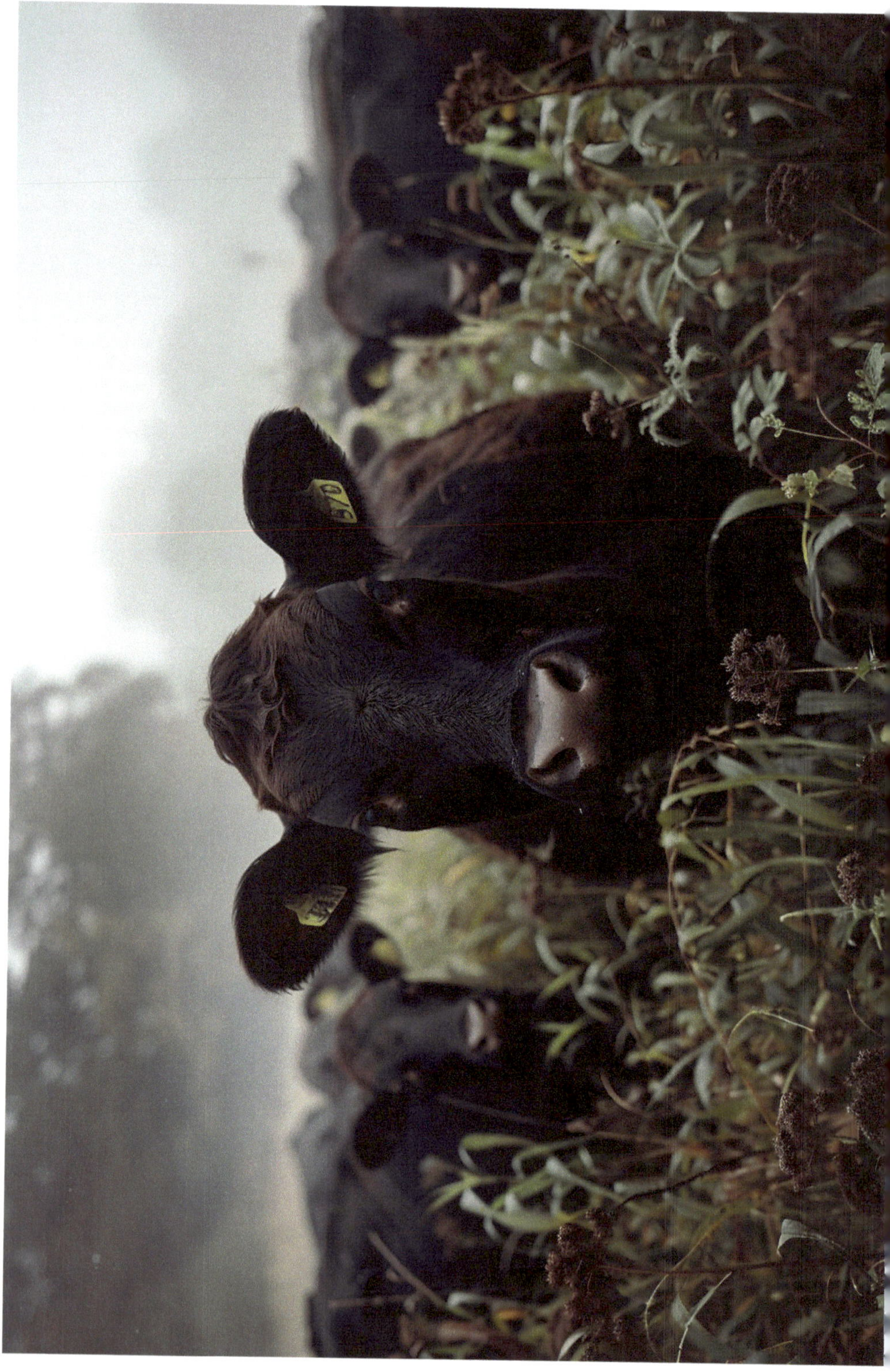

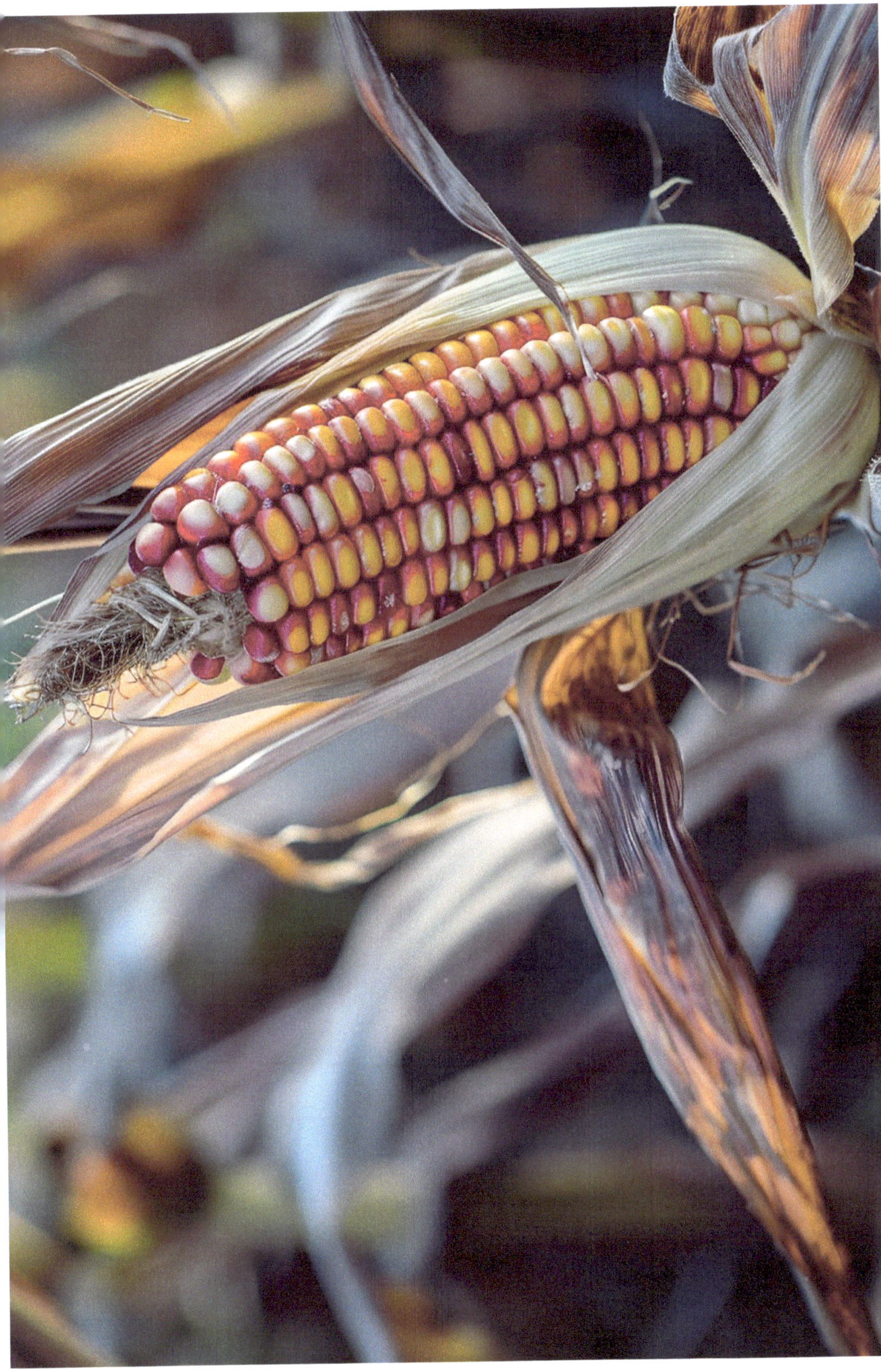

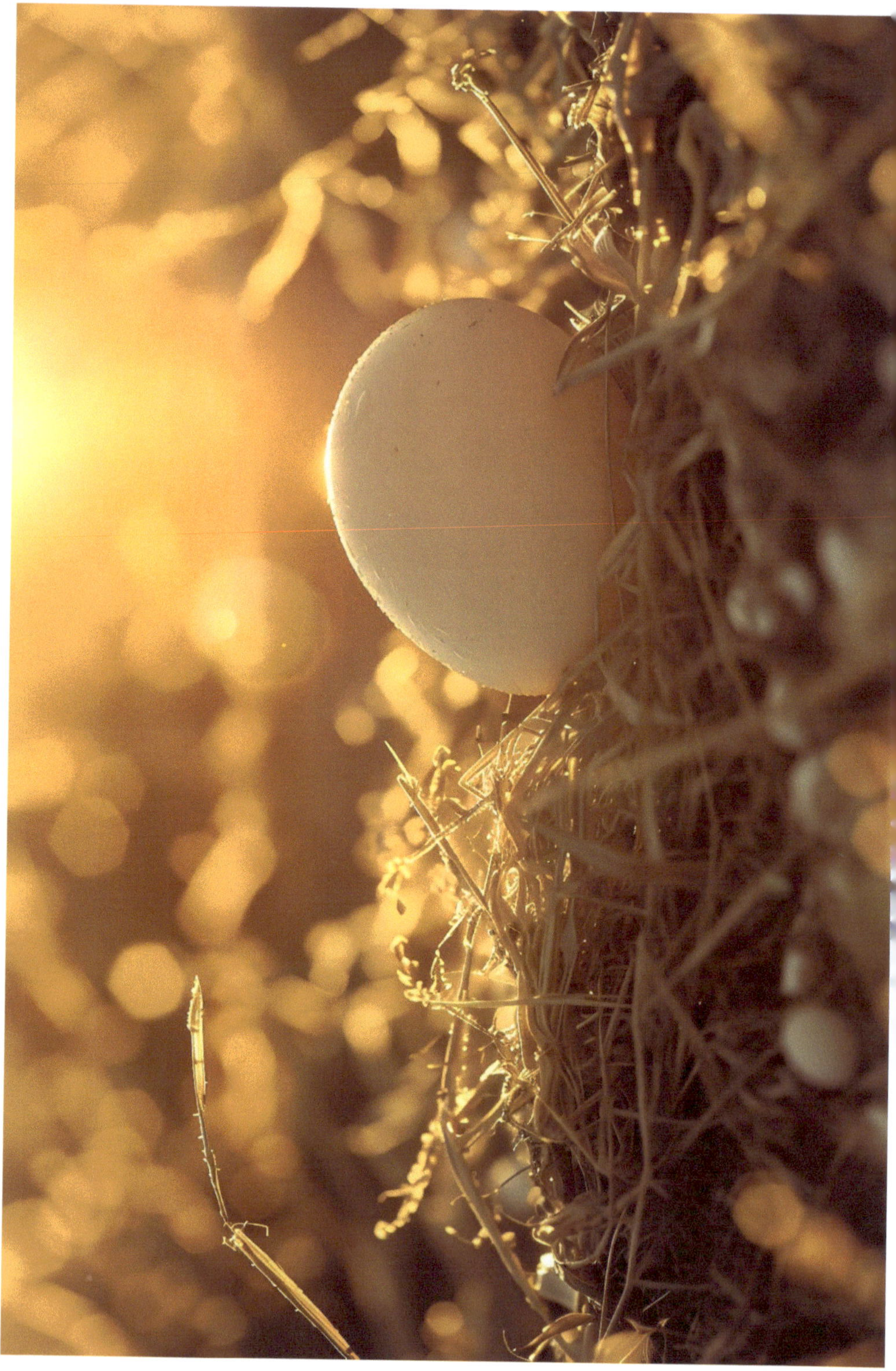

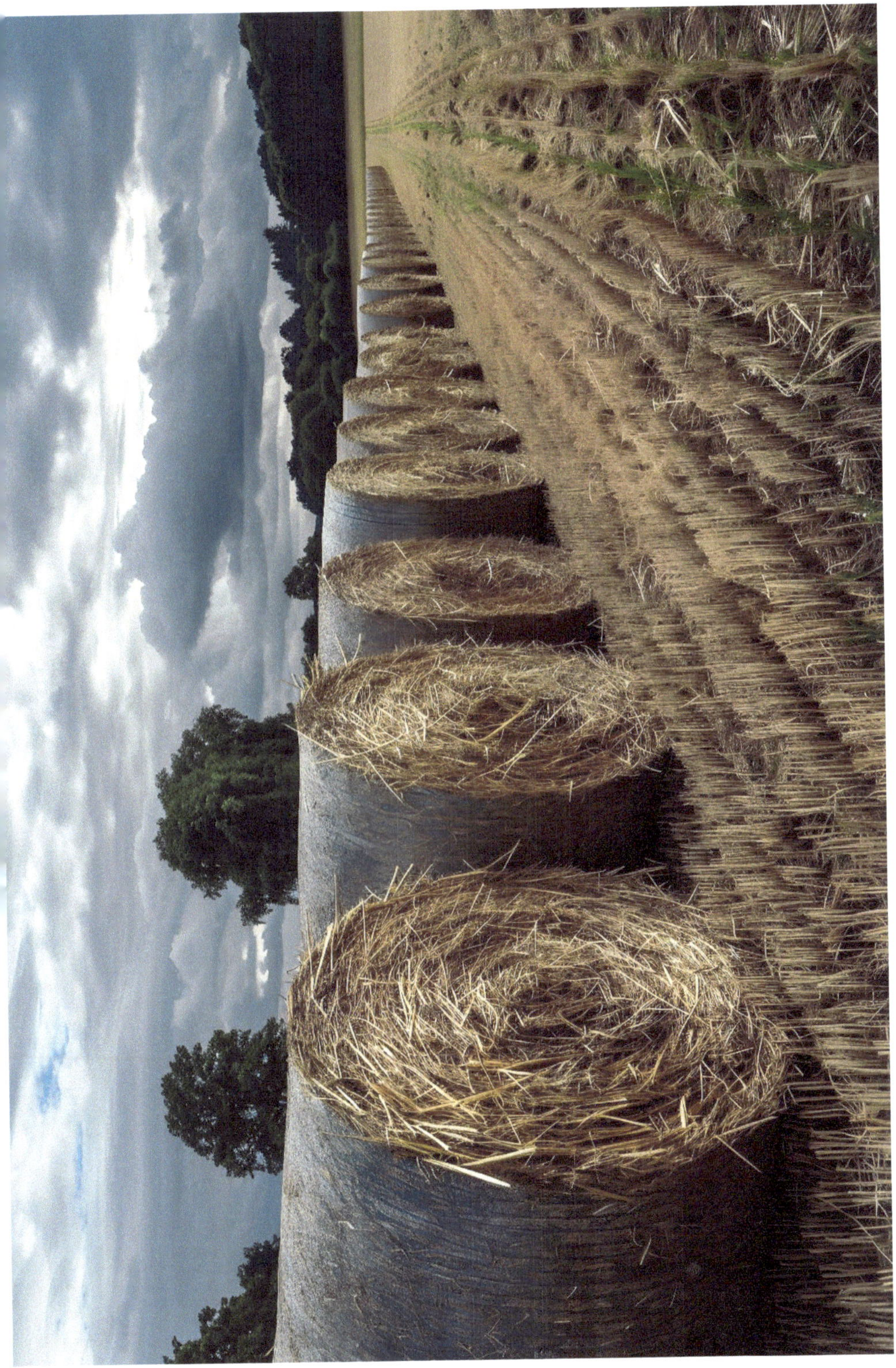

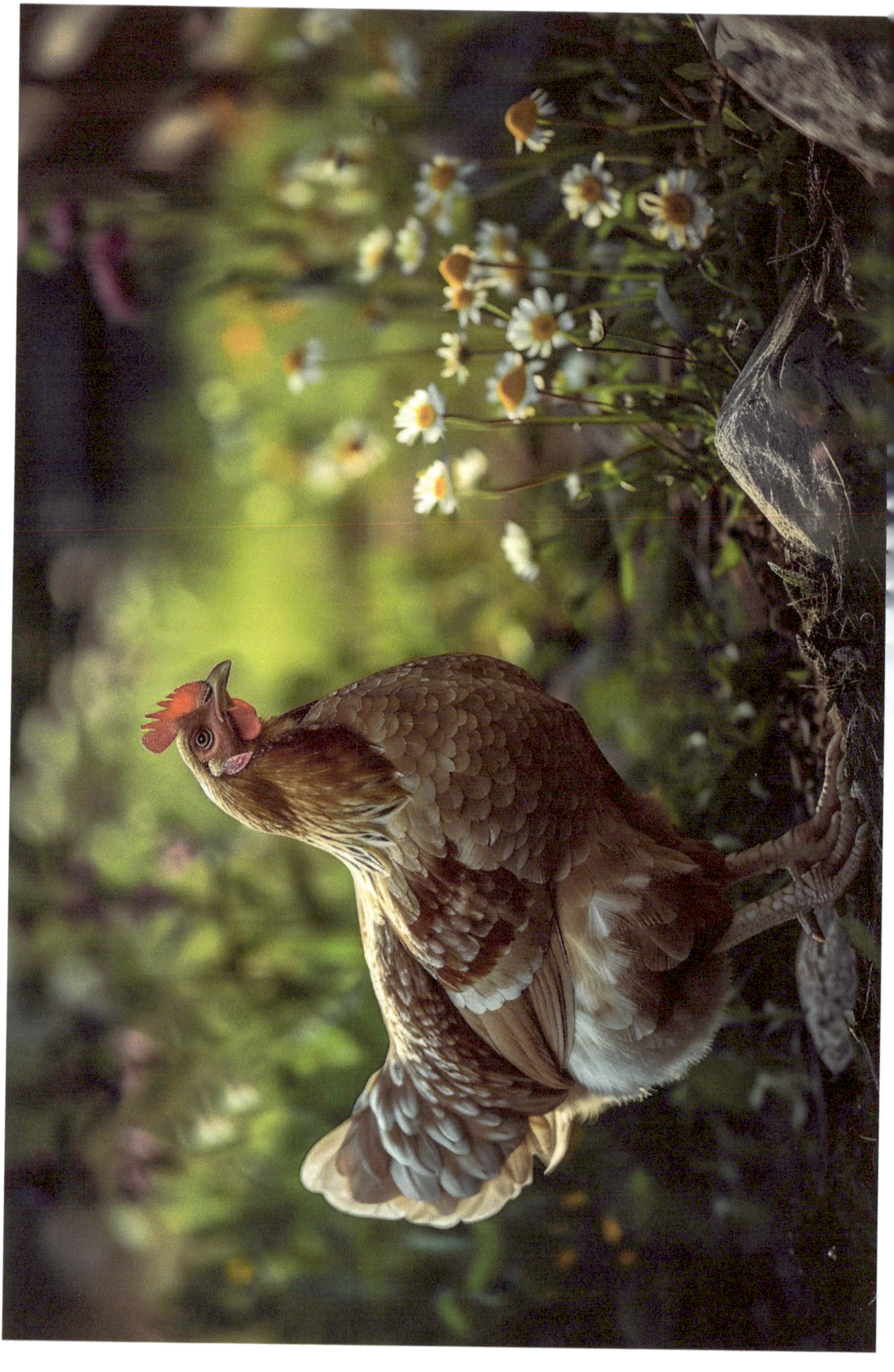

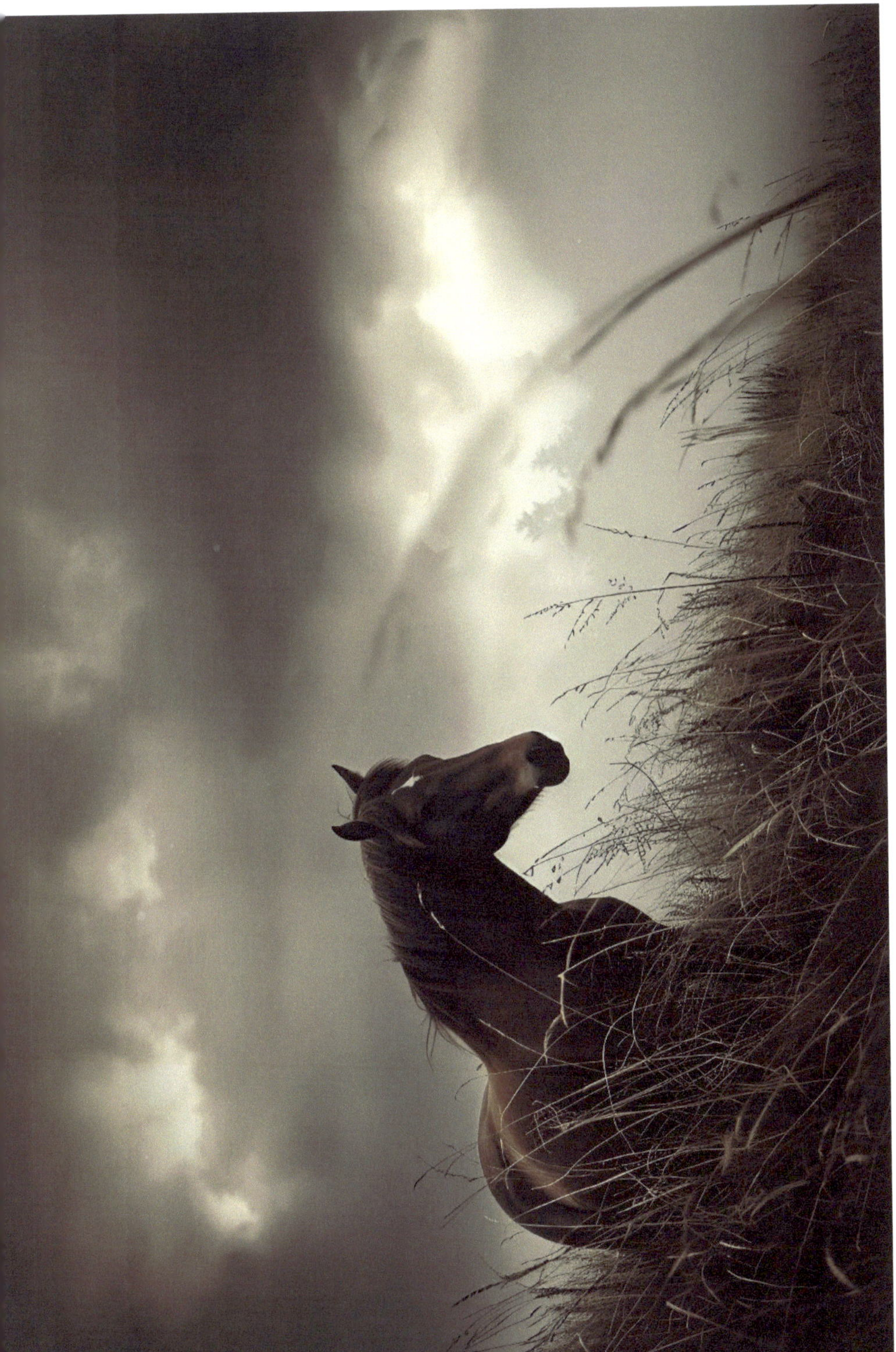

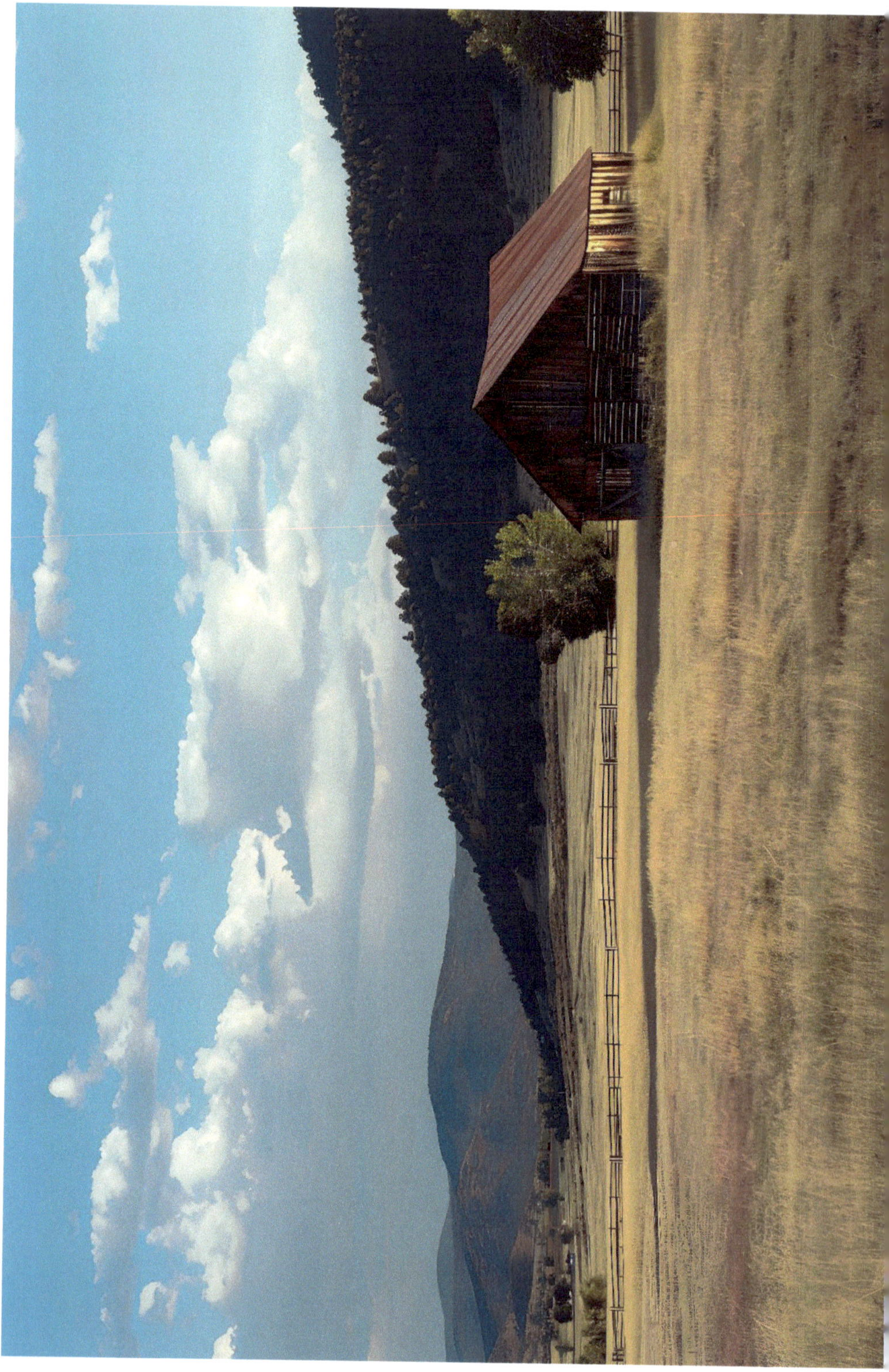

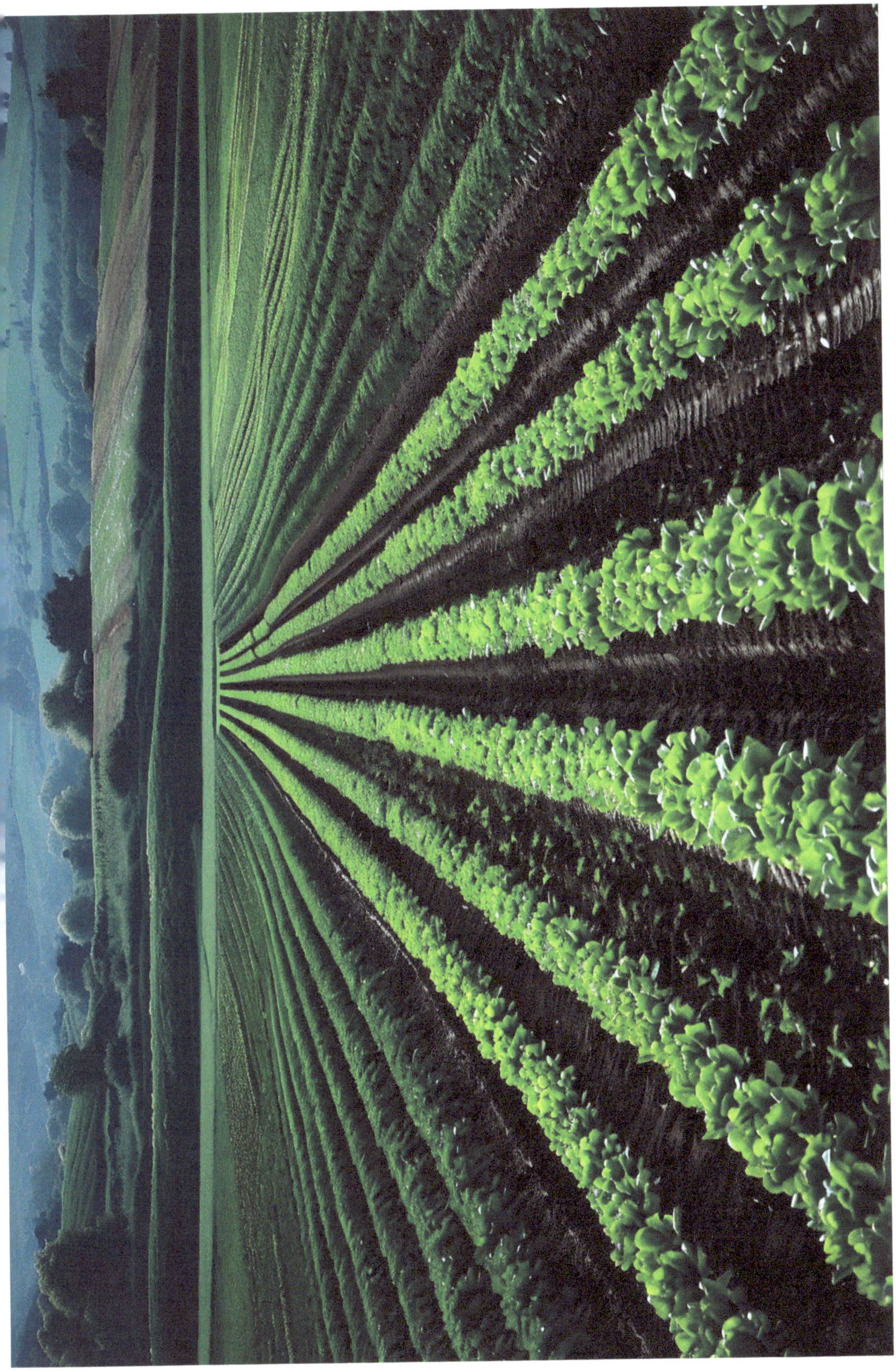

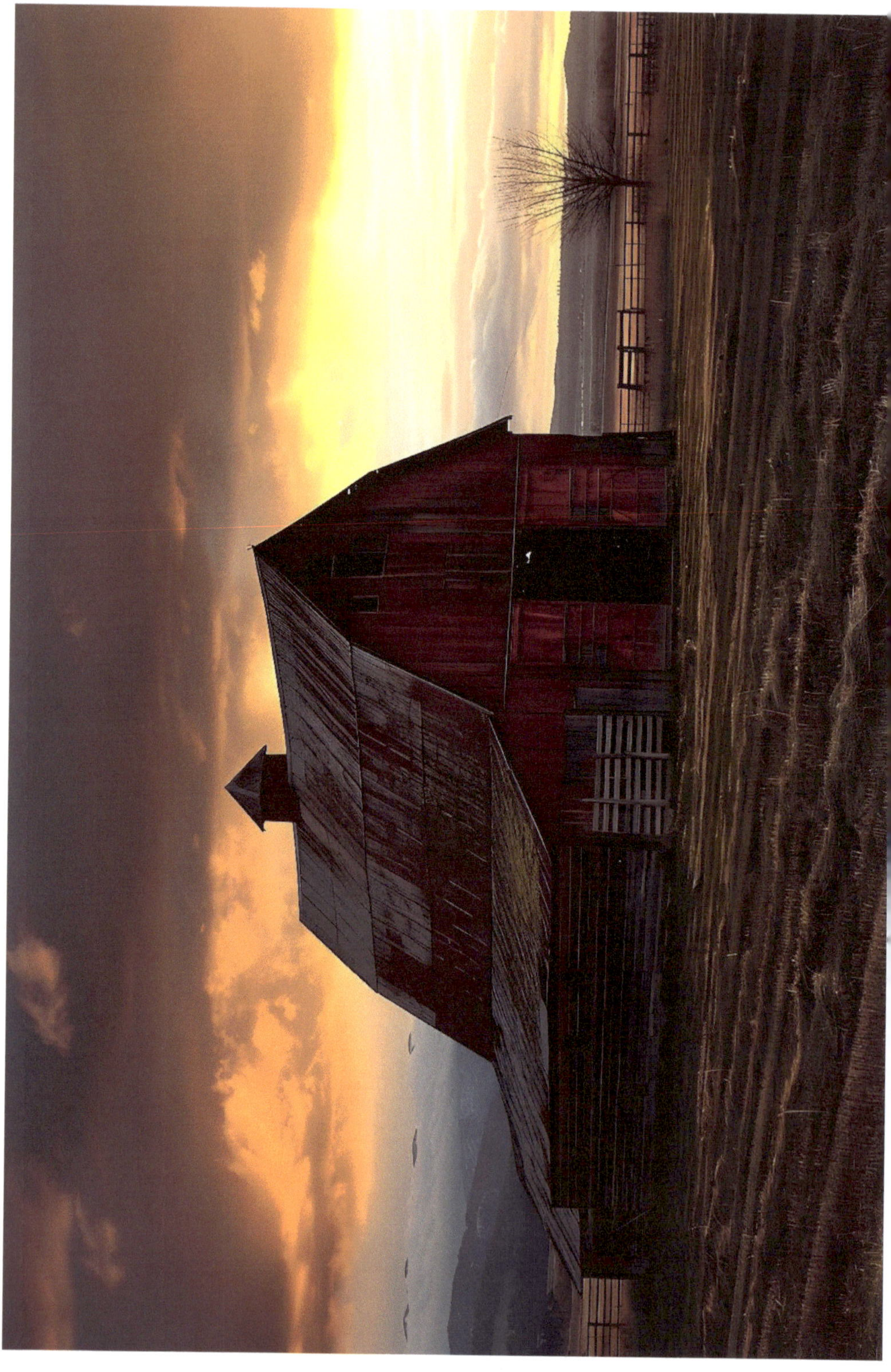

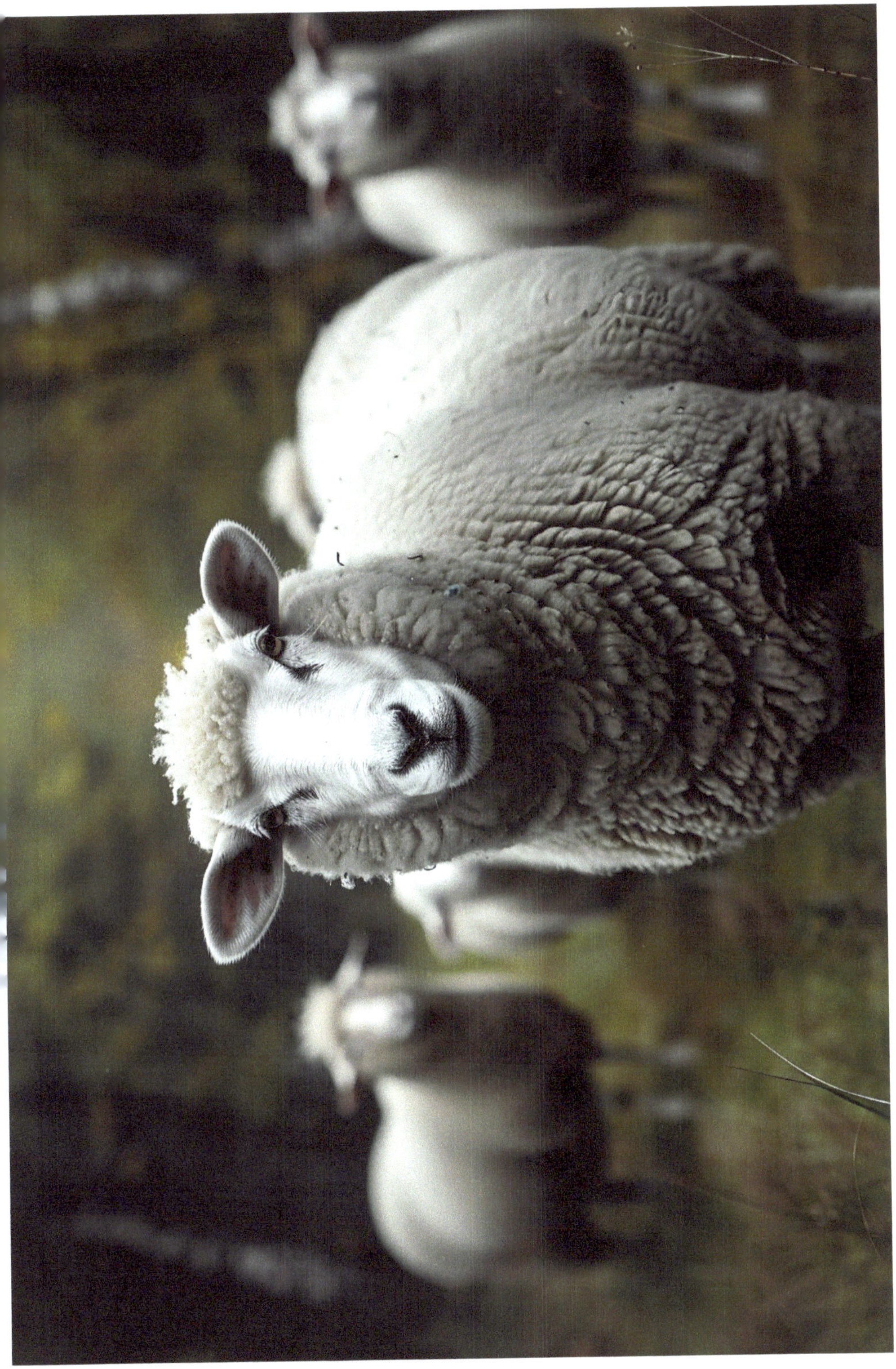

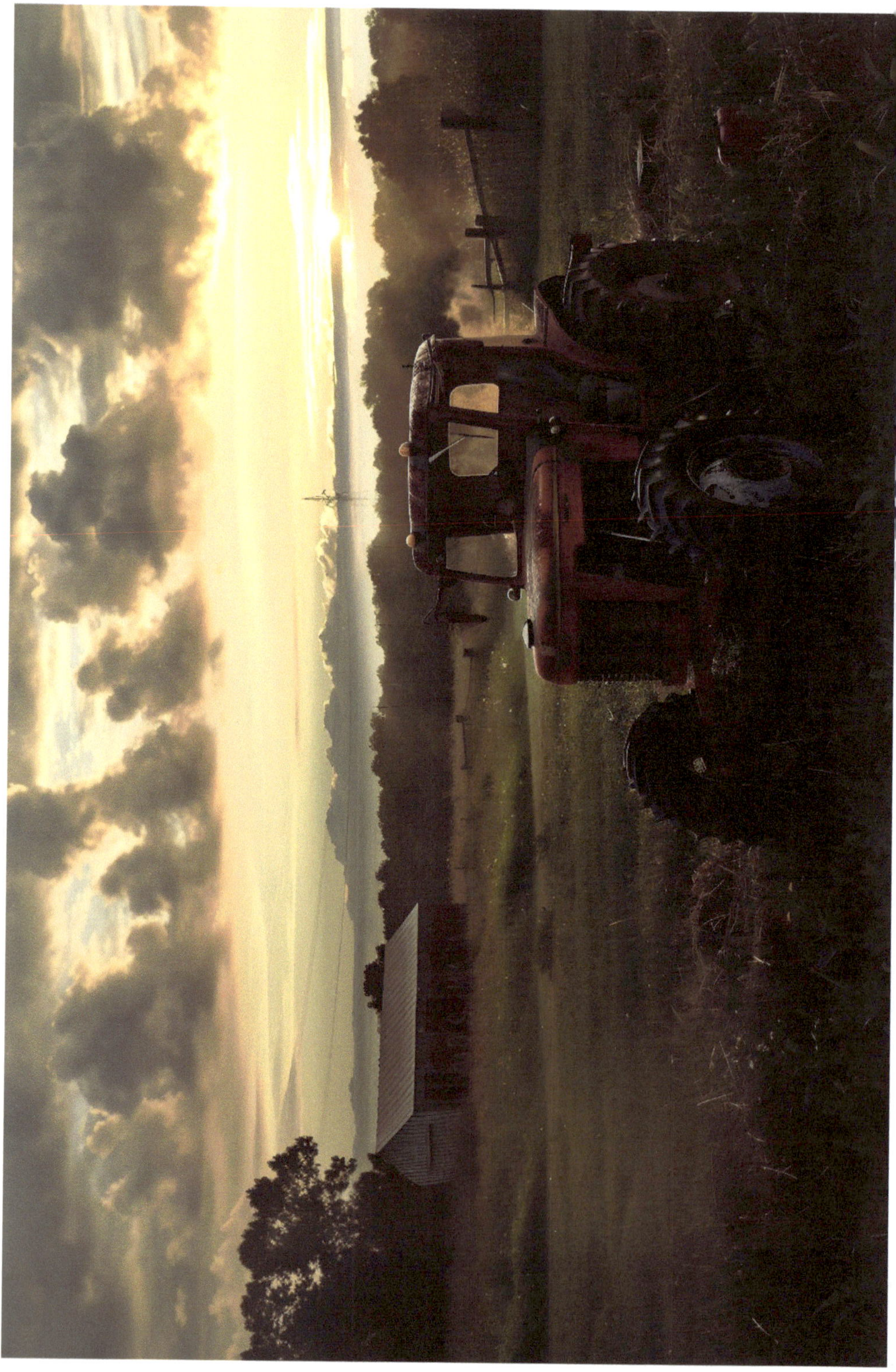

www.ingramcontent.com/pod-product-compliance
Lightning Source LLC
Chambersburg PA
CBHW040759240526
45474CB00008B/114
9798325210488